Callslip Request

Item Barcode:

Call Number: 709.41 S478a
Author: Saatchi Collection.
Title: Sensation : young British artists from the Saatchi Collection / [essays by] Brooks Adams ... [et
Enumeration:
Year:
Location: Main Stx

Patron Name: MOTOKO FURUHASHI
Request date: 2/18/2010 08:51 AM
Patron Barcode:

2 0 1 1 5 8 9 8 2 6 8 5 9

Reply to Reader: Item is not available...
___At Bindery: Seeking next available
___Item Charged Out: Seeking next available
___Damaged: Seeking next available
___Local Circulation Only: Seeking next available
___Missing/Not on Shelf:Seeking next available
___Noncirculating Item: Seeking next available

Request number:

1 3 5 7 7

MOTOKO FURUHASHI

D1228067

2001

2001

SENSATION

YOUNG BRITISH ARTISTS FROM THE SAATCHI COLLECTION

SENSATION

Brooks Adams

Lisa Jardine

Martin Maloney

Norman Rosenthal

Richard Shone

Photographs of the artists by Johnnie Shand Kydd

With 179 illustrations, 104 in color

Thames & Hudson

in association with the Royal Academy of Arts, London

Published on the occasion of the exhibition
"Sensation: Young British Artists from the Saatchi Collection"
Royal Academy of Arts, London, 18 September–28 December 1997
Hamburger Bahnhof, Berlin, 30 September 1998–21 February 1999
Brooklyn Museum of Art, New York, 2 October 1999–9 January 2000

Exhibition selected by: Norman Rosenthal and Charles Saatchi
Coordinated in London by: Simonetta Fraquelli

First published in paperback in the United States of America in 1998 by
Thames & Hudson Inc., 500 Fifth Avenue, New York, New York 10110
Reprinted 1999

Library of Congress Catalog Card Number 97-61608
ISBN 0-500-28042-8

Cover design: why not associates
Cover photography: Rocco Redondo and Photodisc

Frontispiece: *Private View at the Royal Academy 1881*, W.P. Frith, 1881,
Courtesy of a Pope Family Trust

Printed and bound in the United Kingdom

Contents

Acknowledgements

Many people have contributed to the organisation of this exhibition and the preparation of the accompanying publication. We are grateful to Michael Craig-Martin, whose advice and support have been unfailing throughout, and to Sophie Hicks for the flair and skill with which she has designed the exhibition. We extend our special thanks to Leslie Waddington and we would also like to thank Jeffrey Deitch; the title Sensation arose during early discussions with him about an exhibition of contemporary art. Richard Shone and Martin Maloney's personal knowledge of the artists' work has been invaluable. Martin McGinn was immensely helpful with the installation of the exhibition.

In addition, we would like to thank the following who have helped with either advice or assistance: Miranda Bennion, Kate Biro, Jenny Blyth, Annette Bradshaw, David Bussel, Sadie Coles, Tom Cullen, Laurent Delaye, Anthony D'Offay, Christopher Ferguson, Michelle Gillard, Lisa Jardine, Allen Jones, Jay Jopling, Sophie Lawrence, Jem Legh, Honey Luard, Malcolm McLaren, Victoria Miro, Alex Myers, Sam Oakley, Maureen Paley, Tom Phillips, Sarah Praill, Anthony Reynolds, Sarah Rogers, Johnnie Shand Kydd, Karsten Schubert, Nicholas Serota, Nikos Stangos, Emma Underhill, Amanda Vinnicombe, Robert Williams, and all the staff of Momart. Above all we would like to thank the artists and Charles Saatchi.

Norman Rosenthal
Simonetta Fraquelli

Norman Rosenthal

Richard Shone

Martin Maloney

Brooks Adams

Lisa Jardine

The Blood Must Continue to Flow

Norman Rosenthal

It is autumn 1997, nearly but not quite the end of the 20th century, and 'Sensation', an exhibition of new British art, arrives at the Royal Academy. Not all new British art, but a good and handsome cross-section of it, courtesy of its greatest single patron and supporter, Charles Saatchi. It is now virtually a decade (a long time in the history of any art movement) since 'Freeze', that remarkably resonant exhibition conceived and organised by the young Damien Hirst and his mates in a warehouse in London's Docklands. That was in the late summer of 1988. Sixteen artists were represented in 'Freeze'; nine of them are participating in 'Sensation'. Some of the others remain prominent, though their works happen not to have been acquired by Mr Saatchi, who collects according to his own taste without feeling obliged to follow the general consensus. One of these artists, Angela Bulloch, has been shortlisted for the 1997 Turner Prize, as have others in previous years, including the first prominent painter of the group, Ian Davenport. A few have inevitably disappeared from view. One thing is certain: the majority of artists in 'Freeze', along with a host of others using similar strategies for making and mediating art, have come to dominate the British art scene. Furthermore, many have made a considerable impact in exhibitions and collections on both sides of the Atlantic and further afield. Whatever happens next, these artists can no more be written out of the art-history books than can the Pre-Raphaelites, the Vorticists, the Camden Town Group – or, nearer our own day, the British Pop artists or the new sculptors of the '60s and '70s, many of whose practitioners are still prominent.

Art arises out of previous art, and recent generations serve as inspiration and spur to new work, which none the less has very different, more contemporary, concerns and perspectives. But as far as international reputation is concerned, it appears that the latest new generation of British artists is having considerably more impact than its predecessors. British art, even since Henry Moore, has always appeared to itself and to the outside world to be a little behind in terms of the language of innovation that is central to any idea of modern art. It is for that reason tinged with a certain indefinable if attractive provinciality. This is clearly no longer the case. Or is it? Perhaps one of the questions this exhibition will answer is precisely that – whether art in Britain, never quite central to the European cultural experience, nor quite radical in terms of the great American art experiment that commenced with Jackson Pollock, can now hold its own as second to none. Can London become the unchallenged centre for the practice and presentation of contemporary art? In the past, Paris, New York and even

Fig. 1 Above • **Théodore Géricault**
Severed Limbs | 1818
Musée Fabre, Montpellier

Fig. 2 Opposite • **Gustave Courbet**
L'Origine du monde | 1866
Musée d'Orsay, Paris. © Photo RMN

Düsseldorf have been able aggressively to claim this role, by virtue of the density of activity in each city over considerable periods of time, with many artists, as well as collectors and galleries, contributing to the debate with originality and daring. If London could now claim such a position, that would be a first, and surely grounds for celebration. Certainly, it can be a full-time job just to keep up with all the exhibitions of new art in London, as anyone who regularly looks at the art listings of *Time Out* can see. There are numerous commercial galleries and literally dozens of artist-run, essentially non-commercial spaces that spring up and as rapidly close down, much like subculture dance clubs. In the East End of London for the most part, these spaces can be almost anywhere. They are to be found in abandoned warehouses, deserted factories, unlettable modern office developments, churches and even synagogues, in St James's in the very heart of London or in Docklands. A street map is vital for tracking down obscure addresses where art made with deadly serious intent is being presented. To follow the art scene this closely is by turns invigorating and depressing, and requires time and patience. Nothing is more frustrating than a long trek to a space, only to realise that it holds little of interest. But next time this will be compensated by the pleasure of genuine discovery. Many of the lesser-known artists in this exhibition have been acquired in this way by Charles Saatchi, who has a patience and enthusiasm for contemporary art that is second to none.

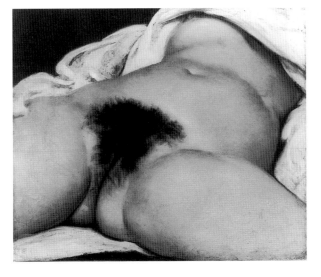

The model for all this frenetic activity was 'Freeze'. By the time the three-part show ended it was already a legend in insider circles. I for one managed to see it courtesy of the persistent young Hirst, who came to collect me very early one morning in a rickety old car and drove me down to Docklands so that I might be back at the Royal Academy by 10.30 am. Art is not just about making a vision; it is also about imposing that vision on others. Hirst was as good and skilful a publicist for his art and that of his contemporaries as he was a maker of art himself. He certainly was not promoting himself as their most significant representative, as the media later claimed. At exactly the time of 'Freeze' Rachel Whiteread was showing her ambitious sculpture *Ghost* (p. 184–5) at the recently established Chisenhale Gallery in the East End. I had not heard of her at the time, but Hirst insisted that I see this and drove me there too. I was greatly impressed with the poetic originality of what I saw. There was at that time, and there happily continues to be, a great generosity of spirit among these artists, who not only show together but support each other in a thousand other ways too. Thus was established a new subculture that became so substantial and widespread it could not fail to be noticed. Naturally art schools played their part. Goldsmiths in New Cross, South East London, was to this generation what the Royal College was to Pop art and St Martin's School of Art was both to the new sculpture of the '60s and the Conceptual art of the '70s. But it is what happens to artists after they leave college that ultimately counts. Hirst's strategy of self-promotion, fully grounded on the originality and strength of what was being made, quickly paid handsome dividends.

Norman Rosenthal

This was of course not the first time that artists have taken the initiative of self-promotion, not waiting for critics, collectors, dealers or museum curators (they least of all) to secure their first step on the ladder to immortality that somehow or other is the aim of every artist. Art first must be conceived, second executed and third presented to a public, however small, before it stands a chance of entering the general vernacular. In France in the 19th century, Géricault (fig. 1), Courbet (fig. 2), Manet or the Impressionists were all enterprising artists imposing themselves on an unwilling audience. The same is true of the great art movements of this century. They were made up of artists producing work that the public for art neither wanted nor expected, but were forced to swallow because it raised issues of modernity that could not be avoided. That reluctant audience included critics and collectors, and even older artists, who inevitably feel their own pre-eminence threatened. Who, after all, is not made to feel uncomfortable by the unknown in art, as for that matter in all things? It is natural and easy to fall in love with what is preconceived to be right and proper, good or beautiful. We now all love the Impressionists because we have come to know and thus feel comfortable with them. But the chief task of new art is to disturb that sense of comfort.

So what is so new about the art in 'Sensation'? Why has this art had such a public resonance, unparalleled in this country since the arrival of the Pop generation, many of whom of course are now distinguished members of the Royal Academy? The answer lies surely in this generation's totally new and radical attitude to realism, or rather to reality and real life itself. They combine this with a complex knowledge of recent art developments in Britain and further afield, which they ambitiously wish to challenge and extend. A visitor to this exhibition with an open mind and well-developed antennae for life and art will perceive an uncommonly clear mirror of contemporary problems and obsessions from a perspective of youth. Presented with both seriousness and humour (often black), and in an extraordinary diversity of materials and approaches, both traditional and unexpected, these works serve as memorable metaphors of many aspects of our times. Some of these aspects are shocking, and are by many of us all too willingly swept under the proverbial carpet in our endless search for that elusive thing called beauty. Why were Manet's *Olympia* or the *Déjeuner sur l'herbe* (fig. 3) such an outrage to contemporaries? Because by taking themes and compositions that had acquired the respectability of tradition, in his case from the Renaissance, Manet drew attention to contemporary and even sordid problems. He did so with aesthetic refinement, but also with naked sensation every bit as attention-grabbing as that of his contemporary novelists or political commentators.

The art gallery is a public place where we cannot so easily keep our thoughts and blushed embarrassment to ourselves, unlike in the darkness of the theatre or cinema, or the privacy of reading. Visual artists for this very reason have a peculiar ability – and therefore, whether they like it or not, a responsibility – to draw attention to that elusive thing we call reality, which

may, when fused with fantasy and personal obsession, bring forth something that can be recognised as art. In this exhibition we can witness and engage with metaphors of sensations, positive and negative, that remind us of big issues of our time, often of *all* time: love and sex, for instance, or fashion and food, waste and plenty, boredom and excitement, child abuse and violence, disease, medicine and death, shelter and exposure, science and metamorphosis, simplicity and complexity. The art of our century has continually confronted its audience with a series of dislocations that are meant to be enjoyable and, in equal measure, to jolt us out of our complacency. In our times all ways of making art, old and new, are legitimate. Painting and sculpture as traditionally understood are as valid as installation, performance and high-tech methods of producing images to lodge in our minds. No one looking at this exhibition could possibly claim that painting is dead. Whether figurative, ornamental or pure abstraction, contemporary painting is very much alive, and includes work on the grandest scale – paintings that show the human figure from new and extraordinary perspectives, and that mean to unsettle us as we look together with our chance neighbour in the gallery at things normally seen in private. It has always been the job of artists to conquer territory that hitherto has been taboo. Goya made art out of the ghastly horror of war (fig. 4); his etchings have not quite lost their ability to shock. And Hieronymus Bosch's *Garden of Earthly Delights* (fig. 5) has retained its power to make us conscious of our own fantasies and suppressed desires. But in time even such powerful images as these become assimilated, their impact diluted. Artists must continue the conquest of new territory and new taboos.

The greatest images are those that invoke both reality and sensation. Today the young mind and eye continue to seek revelation and self-knowledge. In this exhibition we have the chance to feel and empathise with a great many of our current obsessions. All our five senses come into play – touch, taste, sight, sound and smell are all present in fact or by implication. Equally, here are meditations on time, space, colour and form, the timeless concerns of art. The strange, the mysterious, the freakish, the fantasy of science, the abnormality of the normal and the normality of the abnormal: all are celebrated through the creativity of young British artists. The greater part of this art has been actively encouraged and brought together by a single patron and collector, who himself recognises through art the fundamental absurdities of existence and yet sees it as imperative that the creative life should continue. In recognising this rich and fertile vein, he has done an extraordinary thing. The danger, as always with new approaches to art, is that it descends into production without imagination. The blood must continue to flow. 'Sensation', at this august institution, the Royal Academy of Arts, must not represent an end. It should act rather as a platform that will open a larger public's eyes to a scene in which all are welcome to participate if they wish, as artists first and foremost, but also as collectors, promoters and, equally importantly, as enthusiastic supporters and observers. Contemporary art is a club well worth joining.

Norman Rosenthal

From 'Freeze' to *House*: 1988–94

Richard Shone

'These things are done in gangs', wrote Walter Sickert, 'not by individuals'.[1] He was referring to the way groups of artists not only evolve a particular style or hit on a similarity of content but also to how they introduce their work to its public. A core of artists in the present exhibition have known each other from student days and are closely associated in the public's mind as a 'gang'. On numerous occasions many have collided in fortuitous groupings, corralled to demonstrate a theme or tendency in recent art. Some are bound by ties more intimate than long familiarity as student friends or participants. The public image of a group, however, does not preclude cool cordialities and suspicions among its 'members'; they can 'hint a fault, and hesitate dislike'; and they can utterly condemn. Some work in almost secretive solitude; others collaborate with each other, swap and share studios, look to each other for support, have their overlapping interests and sensibilities. But in 'Sensation' as a whole, where several exhibitors are internationally celebrated, others are still little known; and where some are long-standing friends, others have never met. In spite of all these differences, a connecting link is found in the preponderance of artists who attended Goldsmiths College in London, where the impact of the teaching in the 1980s produced a remarkable generation. Their example and several important early shows that they themselves devised became a source of energy that affected a mass of students in other schools and paved the way for the current, seemingly unstoppable exposure of new British art.[2]

To trace the entwined histories of these artists over the last decade or more is like searching for the source of a river: one knows it is roughly in one area but finding how the first trickle comes about, and where it is swelled by tributaries, needs careful reconnoitring. There are the expected elements: the pressures of recent history and the moulding of education; a shared aesthetic climate; social ties; the complex interaction of artists in an established art world and their attempts either to join it or to substitute their own values and a new system. Any close look at this history reveals differences and contrasts more extreme than any features that constitute a common ground. It would be hard to find, for example, two painters so opposed in aims and methods as Fiona Rae and Jenny Saville; objects so contrasting as those by Rachel Whiteread and Jake and Dinos Chapman; or sensibilities so divergent as those of Marc Quinn and Sarah Lucas. Such differences reflect the seemingly unlimited range of options available to artists at the end of the century. It is these varieties of approach, intention and realisation that, paradoxically, bind the artists together. All are connected by new or re-inflected, often radical content that, for most of them, has demanded formal and material innovation. This may sound like a familiar enough recipe, but it surely holds good for the striking range of materials seen here and for layers of feeling and reflection either previously unexamined or thought to be invalid within the context of art. A common accusation from detractors of these artists over the last few years has been that their work is not really new, that it constitutes an abject recycling of recent, fashionable practice to no particular purpose. Its critics point to influences from Dada and Marcel Duchamp, from Arte Povera, Joseph Beuys and Bruce Nauman, to Minimalist pilferings and Conceptualist thefts. But art has always been an evolving language, its words reordered, tailored, quoted and expanded to embody new meanings and feelings. Influence is not pastiche. Nauman cast the space beneath a chair, and so has Rachel Whiteread; Koons suspended objects in vitrines, and so has Hirst; but the ends are entirely different.

What does it mean to be 'new' in Britain? The epithet has cropped up constantly in relation to art, literature and theatre in the last decades. Considering the lack of a Modernist tradition in Britain, this is curious. 'New' becomes a rhetorical device, a convention, and self-conscious novelty is the most traditional of strategies for getting noticed. For 'new' we must nearly always substitute 'current' or 'fashionable' or 'present day' when applied to episodes in British culture. It has rarely implied 'Modernist', as it has in Continental European countries or in the United States. Looking back over the undulating foothills of 20th-century art in Britain, there have been moments of unexpected newness but, with the best will in the world, they do not take their place in the historic narrative of international Modernism. It would have been virtually impossible for a British artist to have written, as did Camille Pissarro to his son Lucien in 1898, contrasting the French and British schools: 'We have today a general concept inherited from our great modern painters and thus we have a tradition of modern art, and I am for following this tradition while we inflect it in terms of our own individual points of view'. The exhibition 'Modern Art in Britain 1910–1914', seen in 1997 at the Barbican Art Gallery, London, showed the exhilarating impact of recent, predominantly French, art on home-grown practitioners of the period. It led to innovations that were dramatic within the limitations of British art at the time, but which, no matter how breathlessly up-to-date or socially vivid, are hardly of significance to the evolution of a Modernist art. The old subjective and humanist basis of British culture remained virtually intact, sieved through its own pragmatic and empiricist approach to creativity. Realism and subjectivity maintained their pre-eminence over the 'formal self-criticism and theoretical debate which sustained European modernism'.[3] Glimpses of something more rigorous are to be had from the Vorticism of Wyndham Lewis and colleagues such as Edward Wadsworth and David Bomberg. But their ultimately humanist aesthetic – in spite of much flag-waving to the contrary – returned them, after a brilliant flutter, to more insular traditions of picture-making.

Richard Shone

The domestication of Modernism is almost the whole history of 20th-century British art. When rigorously undomesticated, as in the 1930s abstraction of Ben Nicholson, it was often seen as purposeless and function-less; in its self-referential restraint, it lacked, its critics complained, human interest and moral uplift. The work of Henry Moore gained swifter acceptance because of its obvious figuration, although the supposed humanity of his sculpture was frequently overstressed at the expense of his formal innovations. Much more to British taste was the individual – and, by implication, communal – voice of an artist such as Stanley Spencer, who in his person and painting represented the British audience's fond image of the artist as eccentric, a little mad even, but fundamentally harmless; the radicalness of some of his content was underplayed. Such singular figures are seen as less disturbing than artists who are part of a movement or group, whereby values and ideas are shared and thus riskily infectious. The innate inability to take Modernism on board or generate an indigenous branch of it accounts for the low temperature of the run of 20th-century British art. But it can also explain some of its successes: foreign dress on loan can be outclassed by res-olutely native style.

The 1950s saw a de-insularisation of British culture, an inevitable reac-tion to the war-bound 1940s. The Constructivists (Victor Pasmore, Kenneth and Mary Martin and others) drew on American and French theoretical principles but in practice remained puritanically understated; some of the St Ives painters entered a fruitful but often ambivalent dialogue with American abstraction; and the Independent Group, with its distinctly urban com-plexion, explored communications, advertising and popular culture with provocative élan, helping to establish the climate in which Pop art flourished in the following decade.

In early 1965 the Walker Art Center in Minneapolis mounted an exhibition to acknowledge a generation of young British artists and the cultural vitality of London. Inevitably the show was called 'London: The New Scene'. This hospitable gesture, the first of several, conveyed to an American public what impact its own art, highly visible in London, had made on native talent.[4] It included a range of artists, figurative and non-figurative, to present certain components of recent British art – Situation abstraction, Op art and Royal College Pop – as the efflorescent productions of a 'hip', anti-establishment, urban scene. This and other similar shows helped promote the now semi-mythical status of the '60s as a golden age. Almost exactly thirty years later, much the same programme was behind the Walker Art Center's 'Brilliant! New Art From London' of 1995, which included many of the artists on view in 'Sensation', particularly those associated with Goldsmiths College.

The 1965 American curatorial enterprise owed much to the successive 'Young Contemporaries' exhibitions and the 1964 'New Generation' show at the Whitechapel Art Gallery. In his catalogue introduction to the latter, David Thompson wrote of the exhibitors as 'starting their careers in a boom-period for modern art' and that British art was 'seriously entering the international lists and winning prestige for itself'.[5] It had 'woken up out of a long provincial doze', sentiments echoed by Herbert Read the following year in relation to the Hampstead artists of the 1930s, such as Moore, Hepworth and Nicholson, who had emerged, he wrote, from a century of 'slumbering provincialism'.[6] Both overstated the comatose to emphasise the new. A vivid mythology evolved, inextricable from the optimism of the period, around the Royal College graduates. In the following decades, art colleges became glamorous tags identifying the rapid succession of groups and movements, with Corsham, Newcastle, St Martin's and Goldsmiths winning high profiles. Dealers and collectors foraged among the degree shows in their homage to youth. Galleries opened on the strength of this 'boom' (fifteen in London in 1961), critics made reputations as apologists, little magazines flourished, and publicity for artists such as Peter Blake, Allen Jones and David Hockney was of the kind reserved for personalities 'in the entertainment and fashion industries'.[7] The era was symbolised by David Hockney's notorious gold lamé jacket and embalmed in the pages of *Private View*. A democratisation of the art world took place that owed much to the art scene in New York, experienced at first hand by an increasing number of British artists, dealers and curators, a transatlantic migration that accelerated a pattern begun by some of the St Ives painters in the later 1950s.

If I have so far focused, albeit selectively, on this phase of British art, it is for the reason that parallels have frequently been drawn between the cultural landscape of the 1960s and that of the '90s. Undoubtedly there are similarities, perhaps more local than international. The 'hip' image of '60s London has its counterpart in the current media picture of the city as the 'coolest' place to be – for clubs, music, food, art and clothes.[8] The gains in material prosperity in Britain under Macmillan and Wilson were echoed in an improving economic climate following the late-'80s recession (though much remained intact from the entrepreneurial pizzazz of the mid-'80s). The activities of the art world and the lifestyles of artists received unprecedented attention in the '60s, as now. The face of London's art world may have changed beyond recognition since the energetic but essentially gentlemanly atmosphere of the '60s, but the progression and expansion set moving then has continued in the same direction. The Institute of Contemporary Arts, the Arts Council and British Council, the Tate and the Whitechapel are all still in place, as are the Royal Academy, the John Moores Liverpool exhibitions and the cycle of the 'Young (rechristened 'New') Contemporaries' shows. Of the changes that have come about, three are notable in this context. Corporate sponsorship of artists throughout Britain is at a level undreamed of in the '60s. The teaching in art schools is infinitely more diverse, producing more sophisticated graduates. And, third, the shift that has taken place in the capital of artists to East and South East London, with Goldsmiths College in New Cross as a determining focal point, has had profound effects.

The fragmented, despoiled, high-rise, war-scarred urban landscape of the East End and Docklands has made an immeasurable impact on the look of much recent art, just as the sights and sounds of Chelsea, Notting Hill

Gate and Carnaby Street can be detected in much '60s figuration. It is the London that tourists, for example, know little or nothing of, glimpsed from a train, with Canary Wharf their only signpost; others have only encountered it in the work of Gilbert and George, in the books of Iain Sinclair and Peter Ackroyd and in Derek Jarman's *Rule Britannia*.[9] It has provided imagery and inspiration for a range of artists – from Michael Landy's street-traders to Keith Coventry's estate paintings, from Rachel Whiteread's discarded mattresses and furniture to Gillian Wearing's *Dancing in Peckham*. East London, north and south of the Thames, has seen most of the cardinal events of recent art, including early shows such as 'Freeze' and 'Modern Medicine', Landy's *Market*, Whiteread's *Ghost* (pp. 184–5) and *House*, Gallaccio's Wapping installation, shows at Matt's Gallery, Chisenhale Gallery, Interim Art, the Showroom, and Sarah Lucas and Tracey Emin's The Shop in Bethnal Green Road.

Behind the achievements of today's young artists are 30 years of solid acclaim for many aspects of British art, particularly since the general removal of Modernist sightlines abroad has allowed for a more liberal climate of appreciation. In North America, Europe and elsewhere international reputations have been accorded British artists of several generations even though all, at one time or another, have been regarded on home territory with a mixture of tired tolerance, suspicion or downright contempt. Caro and Bacon, Freud and Hodgkin, Hamilton and Hockney, Riley and Long, Gilbert & George, Cragg and Deacon have, among others, ensured that never again can British art be sidelined, whatever the foreign critical or curatorial agenda.

Early in 1988, Angus Fairhurst, an art student in his second year at Goldsmiths College, made contact with the Bloomsbury Gallery of the Institute of Education in Bedford Way, off Russell Square. He organised a show there (17 February–8 March) by asking his fellow students to submit work; they included, besides Fairhurst himself, Mat Collishaw, Abigail Lane and Damien Hirst. There was a printed card and an opening with drinks to which several third-year friends came, including Michael Landy, Gary Hume and Anya Gallaccio. This show was a modest curtain-raiser for a more ambitious exhibition, already in the planning for late summer, this time 'conceived and curated' by Damien Hirst with help from several of the exhibitors.[10] 'Freeze', as it was called, was in three parts (Part I: 6 to 22 August; Part II: 27 August to 12 September; Part III to 29 September) and sixteen artists showed work (the painter Dominic Denis, featured in the catalogue line-up, did not in fact exhibit, and an early candidate, Clive Lissaman, withdrew).[11] The venue was the vacated Port of London Authority Building in Plough Way, SE16, close to the Thames, its loan negotiated by Hirst from the London Docklands Development Corporation, which funded 'Freeze'.[12] The show was open four days a week (Wednesday to Saturday, midday to 7 pm), invigilated by a rota of the exhibitors, and a smart catalogue with colour plates and an essay by the writer Ian Jeffrey (Head of the Art History Department at Goldsmiths), commissioned by Hirst, materialised during the run. The LDDC specified that sponsorship would be forthcoming if the exhibition was 'a benefit to the community'. In a letter to the participants, Hirst envisaged workshops for children and pensioners: 'what could you possibly think of to do in an enormous white space with four old ladies, a solid oak table, a meat axe and a stop watch?'[13] Less alarming, organised visits from schoolchildren took place during Part III.

'Freeze' occupies a mythical place in the written and verbal history of recent British art, and the epithet 'Freeze Generation' has become common coinage. The show is regarded as a clinching moment, when Hirst gathered together this remarkable group of second- and third-year students and recent graduates to announce a new direction (figs 6 and 7). It marked, as one critic has written, 'the beginning of a vital period of optimism and enthusiasm',[14] and those people who visited it remember the occasion with fond nostalgia. 'Freeze' has been praised for its professionalism, Thatcherite enterprise and slick marketing; it has been seen as the result of a programmatic pushiness on the part of some of the Goldsmiths staff; as something entirely unexpected of British art schools; and as a riposte to the predominant figurative painting of the decade.

Some of this bears scrutiny. Although several of the artists in 'Freeze', perhaps bored by its legendary status, now downplay its significance, it retains its hold as a prescient event in the story of the period and a tribute to Hirst's initiative. It was not perhaps as professional an operation as is sometimes claimed, and certainly had its share of ad hoc decisions, clashes of personality and much hard graft from nearly all those involved (including cleaning the PLA Building of accumulated bird shit). Some participants even denigrate the exhibits as 'cruddy' or 'feeble'. But the roll call remains impressive. If the work by, for example, Damien Hirst and Richard Patterson has since changed radically, that by Mat Collishaw, Ian Davenport (fig. 8) and Fiona Rae already bore their recognisable signature. Though it seems true that the exhibition was slow to catch on and received scant attention even in

Fig. 6 **'Freeze' opening party** | August 1988
left to right: Ian Davenport,
Damien Hirst, Angela Bulloch,
Fiona Rae, Stephen Park, Anya Gallaccio,
Sarah Lucas, Gary Hume

Richard Shone

the art press, some of the visitors were alert and well placed. For example, an English dealer living in New York, Clarissa Dalrymple, was excited by the show and took that excitement back to New York; this directly led to her curatorial role in a group show the following year at Lorence Monk Gallery (which included a 'Freeze' exhibitor, Gary Hume) and in 'British Art', a breakthrough show in the autumn of 1992 held at the prestigious New York gallery of Barbara Gladstone.

To gain a clearer perspective on the exhibition (and its successors) one has to go back a little. Goldsmiths became a conspicuously successful school of art in the 1980s after a period in which its image was ill-defined, even peripheral. It sought a variety of teachers from the widest possible backgrounds, and enrolled, through perspicacious interviewing, a succession of outstanding students. The Principal, Jon Thompson, was, in the words of his fellow teacher, Michael Craig-Martin, 'a visionary and radical educationalist'.[15] Students were treated as incipient artists from the moment they arrived and the course prepared them for being professional artists after graduation. Thompson abolished the traditional divisions between departments – painting, sculpture, photography etc. – and allowed students to move between them according to choice. But this did not create a mass of free-floaters drifting here and there as the whim took them. Such choice enriched each individual; no discipline was marginalised or materials short-changed; and each student, in consultation with a tutor, structured her or his course.[16] An open-studio system guaranteed a 'volatile visual atmosphere' and self-motivation became essential.[17] At the same time, continual discussion in front of students' work, and intensive seminars and tutorials engendered a high level of critical debate. Many well-known artists taught there over the years, but mention must be made of Thompson himself, Yehuda Safran, Richard Wentworth and Michael Craig-Martin as contrasting and inspirational figures.[18] For the most part, the teachers were visible as practising artists and thus contact was maintained between art education and the

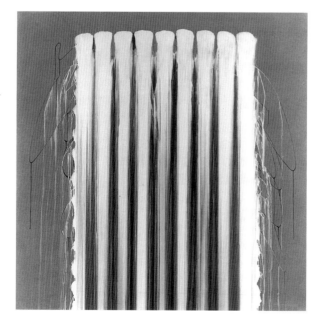

exigent world of dealers and collectors. In the period prior to 'Freeze', recent graduates and postgraduates included Julian Opie, Lisa Milroy, Simon Linke, Grenville Davey, Mark Wallinger and John Frankland. Several had already begun to show in prominent commercial galleries and group exhibitions abroad. This bred an immeasurable air of confidence and expectation in the younger generation. They found, too, that they did not have to fight or skirt around an unsympathetic regime.

Under Jon Thompson's stimulating principalship, Safran's fastidious European outlook, Wentworth's inspirational mixture of the quixotic and the mundane and Craig-Martin's influential practical impact and knack of unearthing true potential, the students had access to a terrific range of options. It is inaccurate to castigate Goldsmiths, as do some detractors, as narrowly didactic in its teaching, uninterested in wider cultural issues and as a battery-farm for neo-conceptual clones. It attracted students exactly because, as Julian Opie has written, it had no constricting 'house style'.[19] Nor were the freedoms it offered self-indulgent or solipsistic; lazy self-expression was not encouraged. At one point or another, nearly all the artists in 'Freeze' had Craig-Martin as their tutor and attended his seminars about their work; many continued to benefit from his advice after leaving Goldsmiths, softening the blow of post-art-school trauma.

In other ways, the students were absolutely typical of the time – poor, enthusiastic, hardworking (with some notable periods of flunk, when the pool-table in the bar was more attractive than the studio). Most were from modest backgrounds outside London; they were quarrelsome, clannishly protective and socially rumbustious. They liked being at Goldsmiths. Those who were to show in 'Freeze' tended to form a flexible but identifiable group within the school as a whole. They were socially and culturally inquisitive. The majority were affected by art from outside Britain (though work by Wentworth, Opie and Craig-Martin, all internationally aware, was important to them). Among the most memorable shows they saw in the 1980s were Joseph Beuys's installation 'Plight' (Anthony d'Offay, 1985), 'Falls the Shadow' (Hayward, 1986), Bruce Nauman (Whitechapel, 1987) and several exhibitions held at the Saatchi Gallery, an exemplary and unique showplace in London, established by Charles Saatchi in 1985 in a stunningly remodelled paint factory in St John's Wood. To visit the exhibitions there was a point of duty for many of the students (group visits and private-view cards from teachers helped); illuminating and influential was the two-part 'New York Art Now' (September 1987–April 1988), which included work by Robert Gober, Ashley Bickerton and Jeff Koons. Here they could find confirmation of, or add to, their own preferences and direction.

The work of the original 'Freeze' artists and their contemporaries manifested a great range of materials, fabrication and content. Painting, however, remained highly visible and has engaged a large proportion of the artists – from variations on the figurative by Wallinger, Harvey, Hume, Ofili, Richard Patterson, Brown and Coventry to the 'abstraction' of Rae, Hirst, Francis, Callery and Martin. The use of existing prefabricated objects, particularly furniture, or subtle retakes on such objects, has been a consistent feature (in Hirst, Lane, Turk, Whiteread, Lucas, Pigott, Wyn Evans, Simpson); categorisation and classification has shaped works by Wallinger, Hartley, Hirst, Chodzko and Lane. One of the knee-jerk accusations from critics of these artists is that their work eschews accessible imagery from daily life, that it is deliberately obscurantist, and that its often cool, ironic, flip or distancing strategies are somehow not sincere or life-affirming. This seems to show a misunderstanding of much past art, a typically British confusion of ends and means and – equally British perhaps – a confusion of values, as touched on earlier in this essay. In addition, the imagery and cultural assumptions of the artists are far removed from the background and expectations of some of the new art's fiercest critics. The multiplicity of content and reference is, in fact, remarkable, if often less portentously up-front than, for example, in some American art of the '80s and '90s. Such reinvigoration of subject matter has inevitably gone hand in hand with the appropriation of new, sometimes unusual materials – from glass eyes, cigarette butts and blood to formaldehyde and fried eggs. All have fuelled, usually in very direct ways, the articulation and transformation of imagery drawn from daily, urban life – a bed, a room, a hospital door, sport, poverty, rural dreams, television, food and death.

Just before 'Freeze', the Goldsmiths MA Degree show, unusually well presented in the Millard Building, the College's Fine Art annexe in Camberwell, had included work by Ian Davenport, Michael Landy and Gary Hume. A few months later (November–December), all three were given a group show by a young dealer, Karsten Schubert, who had opened a gallery in April 1987 at 85 Charlotte Street, W1. This gallery played a key role in establishing the names of several of the artists in the current show and was already a port of call for inquisitive students. Schubert, who was born in Germany, first worked in England for the Lisson Gallery. He began the Charlotte Street gallery in partnership with Richard Salmon, a private dealer who had earlier worked for Marlborough Fine Art. They operated from two floors of an old house in the heart of what has been called Fitzrovia, opposite the offices of Saatchi & Saatchi; the presence of both businesses was indicative of the revived complexion of this once famous artists' and writers' quarter. Initially, the gallery was determinedly international and crossed the generations. German, American and British artists showed there – from classic Modernists such as Dan Flavin to Ed Ruscha and Wayne Thiebaud from California, from young Germans such as Förg, Locher and Grünfeld to maverick British artists like Victor Willing and Bob Law. But its opening show, of sculptures by Alison Wilding, was a foretaste of its role as midwife to the new British generation. Leslie Waddington soon scooped up Davenport, whose 1990 solo show there was the first post-'Freeze' critical and commercial success, to be followed the next year by Fiona Rae's equally auspicious debut. Schubert exhibited Hume in 1989, Collishaw, Fairhurst, Landy and Whiteread in 1990, gave Gallaccio (fig. 9) and Whiteread their first solo shows there in 1991 and Abigail Lane her first

Fig. 9 Above • **Anya Gallaccio**
Preserve (Beauty) | 1991
Window installation at Karsten Schubert Ltd

Fig. 10 Opposite • **Michael Landy**
Market | 1988–90
Installation at Building One, Bermondsey, London
© Michael Landy

show in 1992. The gallery weathered the recession, retaining its buoyant image in a period that saw several new dealers fail. Alongside galleries such as Anthony Reynolds, Victoria Miro, Laure Gennillard and Interim Art, run by the American artist-turned-dealer Maureen Paley, Karsten Schubert swiftly built up a high profile for new British art abroad. It also acted as a social meeting-ground, hosting sometimes lavish openings and celebratory parties, often with an international flavour and mixing up the different generations of artists – from Rodrigo Moynihan and Robert Medley through Richard Hamilton and Ed Ruscha to the Lisson sculptors; and from Tim Head, Alison Wilding, Lisa Milroy and Antony Gormley, for example, to the latest art-school neophytes, usually in black and sporting a stud or earring. Collectors, writers, even curators were drawn to the gallery, and connections and friendships were made that have proved lasting. After the parties there was pavement discussion and *bavardage* through Soho streets in which every other building seemed to be undergoing refurbishment, where every restaurant and bar was full and where every other doorway contained the homeless.

In the two years that followed 'Freeze' the pace quickened, collectors sniffed the air and critics spread supportive words. Among others, Andrew Renton in *Blitz*, Sarah Kent in *Time Out* and Andrew Graham-Dixon in the *Independent* offset the rumbling stormclouds of critical derision and conspiracy theory that were soon to burst in other sections of the press – from *Modern Painters*, first issued at the time of 'Freeze' to promote 'traditional British art' (Heron above Rothko, Hitchens above Warhol), to the pages of the *Evening Standard* and the *Spectator*. In 1990 three further warehouse shows along the lines of 'Freeze' were organised, this time with wide-ranging sponsorship from within and without the art world – 'Modern Medicine', 'Gambler' and the 'East Country Yard Show'. The first was organised by Carl Freedman and Billee Sellman with Damien Hirst; the second, which included two young American artists, by Freedman and Sellman alone.[20] Both shows were held at Building One in Drummond Road, SE16, where a small yard and modest door hardly prepared you for the hangar-like space, then recently vacated by Peek Frean Biscuits. In the first two, Hirst began to show his true colours as an artist, and it was from 'Gambler' that Charles Saatchi acquired *A Thousand Years* (p. 94); in 'Modern Medicine' there was a startling projection by Mat Collishaw, mating soft-porn with crucifixion, in a room of its own seen through a slit in the wall; a bleakly memorable aquatic installation by Craig Wood was in the building's basement. The 'East Country Yard Show', curated by Henry Bond and Sarah Lucas, was notable for the inclusion of work by Anya Gallaccio and Lucas herself. Freedman and Sellman's last collaborative curatorial venture, also at Building One, was one of the spectacular shows of the period – Michael Landy's *Market* (fig. 10). This massive installation below the top-lit ceiling of Building One was a *coup de théâtre*, consisting of nearly 100 works – vertical stacks of brown, plastic bread-trays and market stalls and greengrocers' display shelving, covered in artificial grass. The

quotidian materials, restricted forms and colours, and the packed, rectilinear layout produced, almost against the odds, an effect of intense fascination, a mood that, curiously, was both bitter and exhilarating.

One of Damien Hirst's early and most compelling installations was also organised outside the gallery system (by Tamara Chodzko, the wife of the artist Adam Chodzko, assisted by the private dealer Thomas Dane), and took place in a vacant building, this time in central London (2/3 Woodstock Street, W1). *In and Out of Love* (fig. 11) centred on hundreds of Malaysian butterflies hatched in the steamy recesses of the 'gallery' from pupae dotted over the surface of several white canvases; flowering pot-plants, banked below each canvas, sustained the creatures during their brief existence. In the airless basement room, eight brilliantly coloured monochrome canvases were shown, their surfaces dotted with dead butterflies, whose wings were lapped in pigment as though they had alighted and died there. There were further elements to the show – glass-fronted wall-cabinets containing glasses, for example – but the main installation was menacingly beautiful in its combination of artifice and nature. Animal Rights protesters, alerted to the show, made the crowded, sticky opening even more uncomfortable; the mood became distinctly ugly on the pavement outside.

Almost overlapping with Hirst's show, the Serpentine Gallery in Kensington Gardens mounted 'Broken English' (named from a work in the show by Gallaccio), selected by Andrew Graham-Dixon and the directorial staff. This was the first large-scale gathering in a public space of work by some of the Goldsmiths artists – Bulloch, Gallaccio, Landy, Hume, Davenport and Hirst – joined by Rachel Whiteread (who had studied at Brighton and the Slade) and by Sarah Staton (from St Martin's). It received widespread attention and was called 'the most important contemporary exhibition of the year'.[21] Not far away, at the Anderson O'Day gallery in Portobello Road,

Fig. 11 **Damien Hirst**
In and Out of Love (detail) **|** 1991
Groundfloor installation at 2/3 Woodstock Street, London W1
© Damien Hirst

Richard Shone

'Hide Show Hide', selected by Andrew Renton, brought together Abigail Lane and Sam Taylor-Wood with two contemporaries from the Royal College of Art, Jake Chapman and Alex Hartley. On the exhibition front in the early '90s the Goldsmiths artists soon had a slightly younger generation from a variety of art schools sharing their space; in the general press, however, Goldsmiths still held the monopoly of exciting new art or, from increasingly vociferous critics, was a totalitarian regime responsible for 'the destruction of art education', with Craig-Martin, in Giles Auty's words, as 'a card-carrying hatchet-man'.[22] The conspiracy theory was compounded in 1991 when two of the four shortlisted artists for the newly revived Turner Prize were Fiona Rae and Ian Davenport; Rachel Whiteread, now associated with these artists in the public mind, was also listed. Her turn would come, in dramatic circumstances, but the prize that year went to Anish Kapoor.

Two publishing events in 1991 began to make the work of these artists more accessible.[23] The magazine *Frieze*, edited by Matthew Slotover and Tom Gidley, was launched that summer with a pilot issue bearing on its cover a distinctive butterfly by Hirst (interviewed inside by Stuart Morgan, a highly supportive critic of several of the 'new' artists). It included a transcript of a brilliantly wry tape-recording by Angus Fairhurst and the record of a public discussion between Andrew Renton, Karsten Schubert and Michael Craig-Martin on the international possibilities of the new British art. *Frieze*'s smart graphic design, plentiful colour, regular projects by artists and the sense it gave of diverse and rapid events threw a firework into the dying embers of *Artscribe* and the dim pages of *Art Monthly*. *Technique Anglaise: Current Trends in British Art*, issued by Thames and Hudson and the One Off Press, was edited by Renton and the artist and writer Liam Gillick. The text was a transcript of a conversation between the two editors and Lynne Cooke, William Furlong, Maureen Paley and Karsten Schubert. Twenty-eight artists each contributed specially created pages of illustrations, and most of the warehouse exhibitors were included. The book quickly became a bible for many art students and has proved a useful anthology, but it was not universally liked: Matthew Collings greeted it as 'fatuous and empty'.[24]

A burgeoning international interest now led to several solo and group shows, such as the Aperto section of the 1993 Venice Biennale and the brief showing in November that year at the Cologne Art Fair of works from the Saatchi Collection; a prestigious commission was given to Sarah Lucas by New York's Museum of Modern Art for its Projects Room; and both Hume and Hirst had prominent gallery exhibitions in New York. In Britain the artists became ubiquitous through touring Arts Council shows, the 'Young British Artists' exhibitions at the Saatchi Gallery (patterned on the New York artists' shows that had held their attention only a few years before; 1993 saw a memorable display by Marc Quinn) and the always controversial displays at the Tate Gallery, given over each year to the shortlisted candidates for the Turner Prize (founded by the Patrons of New Art in 1984), an event that publicises recent art more than any other single showcase. The

Richard Shone

Tate itself, contrary to received opinion, was slow to acquire key works by several of the young artists, but many found their way into the Arts Council and British Council collections or entered private collections in Britain and abroad. Regional museums were reluctant to collect representative works, but Southampton City Art Gallery, continuing its adventurous acquisitions policy, acquired pieces by, among others, Whiteread, Lane and Davenport.

In 1994 Hirst returned to curating with 'Some Went Mad, Some Ran Away', a group show at the Serpentine Gallery that put work by foreign artists such as Kiki Smith, Sophie Calle and Ashley Bickerton alongside British contemporaries – Hirst, Lane, Fairhurst, Simpson and others. Hirst's concept for the show, which he had long nurtured, was welcome as one of the few attempts to demonstrate internationally shared concerns and themes. The exhibition pointed up the issue-based solemnity and ponderous effects of some of the foreign artists in contrast to the irony, pragmatism and wit of some of the British ones (and, it had to be said, the comparative weakness of others). As usual, difficulties and controversy dogged the show (Marcus Harvey's explicit paintings were nearly a casualty of censorship), but Hirst's exquisite *Away from the Flock* (p. 98) became, as a result of being vandalised during the run, one of the best-known works in Britain. It shared the notoriety accorded to Quinn's sanguineous *Self* (1991, p. 147) and to Whiteread's masterpiece of public sculpture, *House* (fig. 12), demolished earlier in the year soon after she had won the 1993 Turner Prize amid the massed flashlights of a bemused and sometimes hostile press.[25]

House has now assumed its place in the myth, along with 'Freeze' and *Market* and *In and Out of Love*. None, of course, was intended as permanent, and *House* was made on the understanding that it would be bulldozed. This concrete cast of the interior of an old terraced house in Grove Road, Bow, seemed, on first view, almost an apparition in the pallid daylight of East London, palpable but not quite believable, pale and forlorn against a backdrop of trees and grass. How modest it was, yet replete with associations and memories and toughly undisturbed by the squall of comment that blew around it, widening from neighbours and visitors to the national and international press. At night, in the streetlight, its details, were intensified, revealing more closely the truth of their origins. It began to startle, to take you unawares. Skinned of its precarious physical reality, *House* implanted itself in the mind, an unforgettable image of arrested time.[26]

Fig. 12 **Rachel Whiteread**
House | 1993 (destroyed 1994)
Grove Road, Bow, London, November 1993
© Rachel Whiteread

I would like to thank the following for help of various kinds in the course of writing this essay: Peter Ackroyd, Michael Craig-Martin, Angus Fairhurst, Anya Gallaccio, Damien Hirst, Ian Jeffrey, Michael Landy, Abigail Lane, Honey Luard (White Cube Gallery), Martin Maloney, Daniel Moynihan, Richard Patterson, Julia Peyton-Jones (Serpentine Gallery), Fiona Rae, Karsten Schubert, the staff of the Institute of Education, Camilla Wallrock (Karsten Schubert Ltd), Rachel Whiteread and Gillian Wearing.

Richard Shone

1. W. Sickert, 'The New English and After', in O. Sitwell (ed.), *A Free House*, London, 1947, p. 58.
2. The phenomenon of 'Young British Art', and in particular the mythical status of Goldsmiths College and 'Freeze', have been fully but inconclusively questioned in S. Ford, 'Myth Making', *Art Monthly*, March 1996, pp. 3–9.
3. P. Ackroyd, *Notes for a New Culture*, London, 1976, p. 147.
4. American exhibitions of contemporary British art include *The English Eye*, Marlborough-Gerson Gallery, New York, 1965; *New British Paintings and Sculpture*, UCLA Galleries and US tour, 1968; and *British Painting and Sculpture 1960–70*, National Gallery of Art, Washington, DC, 1970–71.
5. D. Thompson, 'Introduction', in *The New Generation: 1964*, exh. cat., London, Whitechapel Art Gallery, 1964, p. 5.
6. H. Read, 'British Art 1930–1940' in *Art in Britain 1930–40*, Marlborough Fine Art, London, 1965, p. 5.
7. C. Finch, *Image as Language: Aspects of British Art 1950–1968*, Harmondsworth, 1969, p. 9.
8. Among numerous examples, see especially 'London Swings Again!' in *Vanity Fair*, March 1997, pp. 99–144. For an earlier description of London as 'the liveliest city', especially in relation to its young artists, see A. Haden-Guest and N. Parry, 'In your face and off the wall', *The Sunday Times Magazine*, 18 June 1995.
9. For an account of Hackney and the East End as a paradigm of 'the nation's postwar history', see P. Wright, *A Journey Through the Ruins*, London, 1991.
10. *Freeze*, exh. cat., London, 1988, end page. Earlier exhibition initiatives by Goldsmiths artists include a show by Damien Hirst at the Windsor Arts Centre and works by Rae and Gillick at the Fridge, Brixton.
11. Not all the exhibitors were close friends of Hirst: Fiona Rae and Stephen Park (both showing) alerted Hirst to Richard Patterson, brother of Simon Patterson (also showing), who knew Hirst only slightly.
12. Not a former police station as stated in some accounts and in Hirst's letter (Greenwich, 23 May 1988) to the exhibitors (courtesy Abigail Lane).
13. Ibid.
14. S. Kent in *Shark Infested Waters: The Saatchi Collection of British Art in the 90s*, London, 1994, p. 6. For further views on the 'mythical' status of 'Freeze' see S. Ford, 'Myth Making', *Art Monthly*, March 1996, pp. 3–9.
15. Michael Craig-Martin in inaugural lecture as Millard Professor at Goldsmiths College, 1996 (unpublished; courtesy M. Craig-Martin).
16. The Coldstream Report on art education, 1960, had recommended the abolition of the old National Diploma in Design in favour of an equivalent to the University BA Degree, and that art schools should 'devise their own courses and administer their own examinations' (see R. Medley, *Drawn from the Life*, London, 1983, p. 221). But the report also recommended a firm division between the various departments of each school.
17. Richard Wentworth quoted in S. Greenberg, 'Back to School', *The Art Newspaper*, February 1997, p. 26.
18. Full-time staff and part-time teachers at Goldsmiths have included Nick de Ville, Gerard Hemsworth, Basil Beattie, Mary Kelly, Carl Plackman, Bert Irwin, Avis Newman, Leonard McComb, Glen Baxter, Tony Carter, Andrea Fisher and Tim Head.
19. J. Opie, 'Nudes and Tin-Tin', *Times Higher Educational Supplement*, 8 November 1996, p. 21.
20. The two Americans were Steve di Benedetto and Michael Scott. Tim Head, from an older generation, was also included in the show.
21. J. Stock, 'Acclaim for the Class of '88', *Daily Telegraph*, 29 August 1991, p. 15.
22. Giles Auty quoted in I. Gale, 'The most hated man in British art', *Independent*, 10 December 1993 (section 2), p. 23. See also R. Simon, 'This tragic denial of our heritage', *Mail on Sunday*, 20 March 1994. Among the errors in this article by the Editor of *Apollo*, it is worth correcting one, for it is often repeated: Hirst was not a tutorial student of Craig-Martin at Goldsmiths.
23. Another publishing venture of a different kind deserves mention: *The London Portfolio*, Paragon Press, 1992, commissioned by Charles Booth-Clibborn, contained prints by eleven artists: Fairhurst, Hirst, Langlands & Bell, Landy, Mae, Quinn, Taylor, Turk, Wood, Denis and Whiteread.
24. M. Collings in a review of *Technique Anglaise*, *City Limits*, 6–13 June 1991.
25. Establishment hostility to Hirst reached a head when he received the Turner Prize in 1995. The event was characterised in a leader in the *Daily Telegraph*, 29 November 1995, as 'an odious and disgusting scandal'.
26. See R. Shone, 'A Cast in Time', in J. Lingwood (ed.), *House*, London, 1995, p. 61.

Richard Shone

Everyone a Winner! Selected British Art From The Saatchi Collection 1987–97

Martin Maloney

The exhibition 'New York Art Now' shown at the Saatchi Gallery in 1987–8 strongly influenced the interests and style of a group of young London artists. Rejecting an early-'80s bout of expressionist art from Italy and Germany and its watered-down version from Glasgow, this group adopted the methods and procedures of Pop art, Conceptualism and Minimalism, freely adding new meanings to these older forms to make them their own. Through the amalgamation of internationally recognisable artistic styles with a new youth-orientated content, an element of British culture grabbed the attention of the world. The voice of youth was heard in its many forms, staging anger, indifference, boredom and laziness. The works seemed aggressive, the stance certain, giving them an intimidating presence. New artists strolled onto centre stage and, without asking permission, made art as they might have made any other lifestyle choice, showing a British eclecticism, individuality and eccentricity. They quickly found an international audience already receptive to the cultural diversity of British youth through its music and fashion. People looked, liked and understood work that addressed contemporary life head on.

The myth that surrounds this flourishing of British art over the last decade insists that the work is dry and austerely conceptual. But the legacy of Conceptual art – the dematerialisation of the art object, the focus on art's relationship to language, on studies of time and the art of information systems – does not feature strongly in the Saatchi Collection. The achievement of recent British art has been its radicality of content, not radicality of form. This Collection represents the art of ideas with a high visual impact. It enforces a belief in art's ability to show ideas as physical things, and in this manifests a set of attitudes towards looking at and experiencing the world.

Goldsmiths College of Art in South East London was the hotbed of change. Its non-hierarchical teaching programme under the guidance of the artist Michael Craig-Martin (fig. 13) stressed the democracy of material and meaning. The school asked students to make art that had something to say, to make it in a new way, and to engage with the contemporary world. A striking feature of Goldsmiths College is that it produced several successful painters. Ian Davenport, Gary Hume and Fiona Rae all emerged with a cool approach to painting. Their work may look Minimalist, Modernist or Abstract Expressionist, but the mentality is essentially Pop. Large-scale and ambitious, it acknowledges historical precedent yet does something new. Analytical in gesture and controlled in material, these painters approached their work like sculptors. Delighting in their borrowings from the past, they

Fig. 13 **Michael Craig-Martin
On the Table** | 1970
Jessica Craig-Martin
© Michael Craig-Martin

used quotation and deconstruction and levelled high with low. The intellectual climate encouraged the notion that artists could and should borrow, even copy, from other artists, so they did. Working side by side with artists such as Michael Landy and Damien Hirst, who were using found objects and readymades, these painters learned how to make the most of minimal invention. The usual art-school angst was absent, replaced by a more searching cultural anxiety directed towards the problem of how to make art that would represent themselves.

Fiona Rae pieces together her favourite bits from art. She makes paintings from collaged segments borrowed from classic paintings, reassembling them as her own. Her pick-and-mix selection of gestures, shapes and colours emerges looking like a quasi-Abstract Expressionist painting, but one intentionally lacking the original's authenticity. In our age of feminism she shrinks down the strident 1950s masculinity, and, since the cultural climate has proclaimed the death of the author, seeks for her art the aura of mechanical reproduction. At first deconstructivist, Rae isolated elements on a neutral ground, showing off her skills at absorbing, analysing and imitating, at times provoking the viewer to play detective and identify her painted quotations. Her takings apart were done in order to rebuild and recover the beauty of abstract shapes culled from all manner of divergent sources. Over the years she has mismatched many styles and sources without continually having to acknowledge their quotation or appropriation. She paints flat, coloured shapes, circles and stripes familiar from a hard-edged '60s abstraction and adds expressive-looking scribbles and doodles and puffs of paint using colours and patterns from textiles.

Gary Hume's painting changed dramatically with the times, as an early 'laddish' swagger turned romantic. Consistent features in his work are a play between the figurative and the abstract on a glossy, flatly painted surface made from simple colour arrangements. His door paintings had a municipal connotation that challenged the good taste and cultural neutrality of Modernist painting and Minimalist objects. Tapping into the toughness of council estate culture, he upped the ante. Inspired by the new work being made in Los Angeles, he rearranged his clashes of high and low to assert more strongly both popular culture and a handmade appearance. He looked to the gutter but found the high street. He grabbed iconic images from style magazines as well as art history (Kate Moss, a teddy bear, a disc jockey, a woman's head from a painting by Petrus Christus) and gave them a figurative/abstract mix. His use of decorative colour, shape and surface gloss has given his painting a graphic punch with a brash and boastful white-trash underbelly.

Ian Davenport, who showed with Hume and Rae in 'Freeze', makes paintings by pouring paint. They have the look of the ultimate luxury modern item, combining maximum physical presence with, seemingly, minimal effort. Davenport's method of making influenced a wave of young male painters to adopt industrial-like techniques in order to distance themselves from the cliché of the sensitive hand of the artist. A cult of 'new lad' process-painting was born. Its masculinity of procedure and execution is in contrast to the end product: refined and sensitive paintings that play with nuances of colour and surface detail. The process-painters soon began to exaggerate the strut of their procedure. Jason Martin's large-scale monochromes of thick paint, looking like a vinyl record or a car tyre, are made with one sweep of a brush and suggest what it is like to be young, male and in love with consumer culture. Seizing a painting style that gives away very little is, of course, a revealing thing to do. The monochrome – symbol of sophistication, simple beauty and good taste – is used as a stand-in for a designer object, embodying a return to the matt black '80s, and the promise of happiness from that age of plenty. As nostalgic and well groomed as a teddy boy's quiff, these paintings drip attitude. The process of painting is as sophisticated as the finished product, both narcissistic adventures in cool.

Ideas soon cross-fertilised, with artists making their own versions of what was in the air, a healthy exchange that led to an exploration of the components of painting. Fiona Rae and Glenn Brown, each in their own ways, tackled the idea of quotation and expression. Chris Ofili and Peter Davies explored decoration and abstraction. The rudeness of real life thrust itself under Mark Francis's microscope, as gentle paintings of chromosomes gliding gracefully across the canvas in a steely grey light took on the glare of graffiti. Wallinger's perfectly executed horse paintings followed on from Lisa Milroy's paintings of objects on a white ground (fig. 14), but rather than joining her search through shopping malls of shirts, shoes and ties, his change of subject opened a chink in an art-historical past that many have chosen to explore.

Tackling his pick of the past in a surprisingly different way from Rae, Glenn Brown has emphasised his love of painting by copying paintings as a graphic style, giving them the aura of an 'Athena'-style poster. His respect and reverence for art history led him to make copies of past masters, from Fragonard's frothy scumbles to Auerbach's gloomy School of London impasto. Mimicking brushstroke, expressive gesture and fantasy world, his paintings have the look of the work copied, but characteristics and a surface that are recognisably his own. Brown's choice of Dali opened up the possibility of cool painting working with a striking image, and presented the untamed imagination (albeit someone else's) as subject-matter.

Richard Patterson – who, though also in 'Freeze', has developed somewhat later than the others – likewise explores aspects of the history of painting. Packaging most of the impulses behind painting of the last 30 years (including, for example, the work of Richard Hamilton, fig. 15), he restyles them as his own, making original art from quotation and a dreamy nostalgia for aspects of suburban life. A toy motorcycle daubed with paint or a plastic minotaur are painstakingly rendered in a clash of different styles. The impetuous gesture of a freely made abstraction lies next to passages of an almost airbrushed background and to hyper-realistic detail, uniting stylistic differences by an all-over smooth surface. Attempting to make several paintings in one, figuration becomes abstraction and a gestural wildness

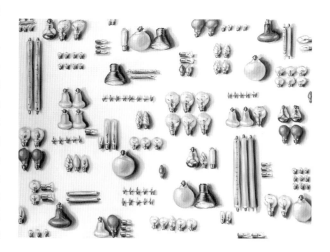

becomes hyper-reality. Patterson's sometimes large-scale and challenging epics have the quality of a film-still from a larger narrative, and leave the viewer uncertain as to which genre each work actually inhabits.

The contrast between Jason Martin's seemingly made-in-a-minute works and the laborious procedures of Patterson and Brown triggered a discussion of the place of skill and effort in the making of paintings. At the same time, the monochrome came shivering back in the work of Peter Davies. Viewed from a distance his paintings appear like the ghost of an insipid monochrome; as one gets nearer, they come alive with intense jazzy colour on a white ground, Pointillistic but with no image. Davies's colouring-in exercise borrows Conceptual artist Niele Toroni's strategy of a repeated single brushstroke, an approach at the opposite extreme to made-in-a-minute painting. A jabbering text-painting listing favourite artists breathes the aggressive punk spirit of an art fan who yet has all the devotion of a connoisseur.

Traditionally, abstraction and decoration sit uneasily together. But the legacy of Hume and Rae found form in Chris Ofili's dazzling use of glitter, dots and dribbled beads of colour. Decorating his surfaces with excessive patterns, using collage techniques borrowed from folk art, Ofili's multi-layered approach challenged the rules of good taste by a skilful combination of eclectic elements. As the decade wore on he pumped up the volume of jarring elements to a louder and more raucous pitch. Playful in realisation, brash in materials, they have a patched-together, homemade look that allows a gentle romantic spirit to animate the cultural mix of their making. Ofili found a way of shifting the art of identity to an apparently neutral form – decorative abstraction, which had not previously been used to discuss issues of racial difference. The work expresses social and political concerns, yet neither coyly requests ghetto sympathy nor affects a gangster-like rage.

The British imagination, haunted by Carl Andre's bricks (fig. 16), has continued to be puzzled by how the Duchampian readymade and untransformed object could be art. Michael Landy's talent first showed itself in the

Fig. 14 Opposite • **Lisa Milroy**
Lightbulbs | 1988
The Tate Gallery, London
© Lisa Milroy

Fig. 15 Above • **Richard Hamilton**
I'm Dreaming of a White Christmas | 1967
Ludwig Forum, Aachen
© Richard Hamilton 1997

Martin Maloney

29

finding and placing of mundane objects to give them an elevated sculptural presence. A stack of bread-crates taken from the street and carefully placed in a gallery space, or a costermonger's barrow festooned with lights and flowers, could through shape, size, surface and material create the impact of a monumental piece of abstract sculpture. Landy made visible the working-class street trader without presuming to explain his world or patronise him. His streetwise stance asserted a political dimension to the readymade and kick-started sculpture to embrace the art of visibility. Sculptors started to refer to direct-life experiences through the objects and materials they used.

Plastic, modern and disposable, Landy's materiality was in strong contrast to Rachel Whiteread's early works in plaster. Her materials referred to the dignity of a past set against the severity of the contemporary world. Modest and subtle, her sculptures were elegant in both material and form. By taking casts of the negative space of objects she found it was possible to copy things from the real world without them remaining seedy or squalid. She often chose objects with downbeat connotations, treading a careful path between misery and squalor. Victorian in their monumentality yet minimal in look, her works were requiems for the residential. Moving away from Landy's Jack-the-lad fascination with the street, Whiteread made sculpture from the domestic sphere with her cast of the space of a room. She conjured up the trace of ordinary lives and used the particularity of things – a bath, a mattress, a light-switch – as a vehicle for collective memory. Abstract yet figurative, unsullied by an excess of detail, her works embody actual spaces from real places. Imbued with all the domestic drama of the home, they suggest loss, decay and change. Not all tombs and sarcophagi, her sculptures are penetrated with the memory of earlier, happier times. The severity of the serious has occasionally been exchanged for a lighter mood, with lilo mattresses cast in coloured rubber. The mundane is made to sparkle, as the fall of light catches the glassy surface of her coloured resin sculptures.

Fig. 16 Left • **Carl Andre**
Equivalent VIII | 1966
The Tate Gallery, London
© Carl Andre/London, DACS/VAGA, New York, 1997

Fig. 17 Opposite • **Cindy Sherman**
Film still #27 | 1980
Saatchi Collection, London
© Metro Pictures, New York

Martin Maloney

30

British sculpture changed with Anya Gallaccio and Sarah Lucas. The lack of material transformation and the apparently effortless means of making expressed a tough street attitude that challenged the well-made art of the home, forcing it into a more direct confrontation with social difference and working-class culture. Gallaccio made a sculpture at the ICA from a carpet of fresh roses left to die. Replacing the substance of Andre's bricks with flimsy flowers, she increased the potential of dematerialised sculpture to hold metaphor, conjuring up an imaginative flight into the English countryside and garden. Lucas's work was very specific. She took Landy's idea of the object as a tool of class visibility and directed it towards herself; manipulating the cult persona of the artist, familiar from Warhol and Koons, she used her own image and posed as a defiant outsider. She became one of Landy's barrow-boy lads – a tabloid-reading, beer-drinking, foul-mouthed assemblage artist. She turned the hard-hitting and unpoetic content of daily life into gently made sculptures, drawing on the material sparsity of Arte Povera and the wit of Surrealism. Landy's laddish attitude was contained in the brutal power of the untransformed object, but Lucas's toughness was softened by her modest and fragile manner of making. Her appropriation of a young, working-class male's interest in violence, sex and alcohol was unapologetic. By adopting it she exposed it. Her work came just at the right time, for the impact of the revival of Minimalism was at an end, and globally there was a movement away from slickly produced objects. Lucas was seen to herald not just a new sensibility for the '90s but a raw aspect of British culture, angry in spirit, grungy in look, cobbled together from a few bits and pieces. Her work rejected the mechanically made and asserted the bare necessities to make a sculpture that amplified a clear and angry voice.

An interest in punk rock turned a traditional sculpture by Gavin Turk – a wax self-portrait dressed and posed as Sid Vicious – into a personification of the teenage bedroom rebel. Mixing the figure construction of a museum waxwork with Cindy Sherman's role-posing (fig. 17), Turk was first on the scene with the British revival of figure sculpture. His focus on self-portraiture has generated a witty variety of ways of representing himself – as a subject for *Hello!* magazine or on a commemorative blue plaque as found on London houses lived in by the famous. His play of egomania was later taken up by Tracey Emin, who fine-tuned the idea of self-portraiture and the cult of the artist by investing her objects, such as her famous tent, with an overwhelming amount of personal detail.

Playing down the materiality of the made and assuming a Peeping Tom, tabloid voyeurism, Mat Collishaw unmasked our shared fascination with sex, violence and depravity. Often using photographic images with strong art-historical allusions, he reveals how past and present picture the weak and vulnerable, locating society's secret thrill in looking at the 'forbidden'. He exposes the complexity of images that are simultaneously revolting, exciting, sexually titillating and boring.

Initially, tabloid culture was approached in an attempt to make class differences more visible. But the fascination with sensationalism quickly grew, shackles were removed and the imagination, like the mad scientist's, ran riot. The discreet thrill of looking at the sordid side of life – a romp with sex, violence and exploitation – was given a no-holds-barred freedom. Such fierce content guaranteed radicality. At the same time, figurative sculpture, with all the traditional concerns of form and balance – as for instance in the work of Allen Jones (fig. 18) – was coming back into the mainstream. Lucas thrust back figuration with her arm and fist in a naughty gesture; Collishaw's soft-core intimacy became full-bodied, enlarged into the sexually explicit fibreglass mannequins of Jake and Dinos Chapman. Heads joined by vaginas, an anus for a mouth, a penis for a nose: the revival of formal figurative sculpture ushered in a quirky mix of children's clothing-store innocence stunted by a sprouting adult imagination.

In Gillian Wearing's world everyone seems to be a freak. She exposes in vox pop photographs and videos the sad tales and tawdry details of mundane lives, presented with all the neutrality and concern of an Esther Rantzen tabloid TV programme. Injecting drama into ordinary life, weaving fact with fiction, she cleverly references TV classics, from Dennis Potter's *Blue Remembered Hills* to the seminal documentary *Seven Up* and the BBC's ground-breaking *The Family*. By raiding the video shelf of '70s TV she has made her own patchwork picture of Britain to prove that 'there's nowt so queer as folk'. Wearing's use of the documentary is not a revival of the neutral stance of Conceptual art, but an advancement in content. Not all have followed such explicit paths. Whiteread's social commentary and monumental solemnity, as in *Ghost* and *House*, inspired many. She pioneered a vein of concern with housing and the poor. Keith Coventry painted Russian Constructivist style paintings using Modernist-looking maps of blocks of council flats, as well as introducing the white monochrome to re-present a polite, old-fashioned idea of '50s Britain, all quaint customs and traditions. Tracey Emin took a different spin on housing and went camping. Langlands and Bell were concerned with architecture and city planning, and made miniature models to expose the power structures encoded in buildings. Alex Hartley looked at the downfall of post-war British idealism and, believing that a minimal object could actually say something of relevance, placed a photograph showing the collapse of the tower block Ronan Point in a sculpture.

Gentlemanly good behaviour went out as the sound of the suburbs took hold. It was the desire to show what happens inside the home that impelled many artists to a particularly British mix of shabby sex and smutty jokes. Marcus Harvey combined an Intimist's painterly decoration, the energetic handling of De Kooning's expressionism and Caulfield's deadpan use of outline to paint images of readers' wives from pornographic magazines. His painting of the iconic image of the bouffanted blonde '60s child-killer Myra Hindley, made of repeated printings of children's hands, put pain into Pointillism. Sarah Lucas made a splash with a sequence of photographs of a lad pretending to ejaculate with the frothy spray from a beer can. For a while the rawness and rudeness of a kitchen-sink realism won out.

Fig. 18 Above • **Allen Jones**
Table | 1969
Ludwig Forum, Aachen
© Allen Jones

Fig. 19 Opposite • **Jeff Koons**
One Ball Total Equilibrium Tank | 1985
Saatchi Collection, London
© Jeff Koons

Developed by Richard Billingham into fly-on-the-wall photographs of his working-class family, council-house life dropped its tabloid mediation for a frank exposure of life on the inside. Whiteread unwittingly opened a can of worms with her penetration of the domestic sphere. Numerous artists fought to find a space to tell the world what British life was really like.

Sam Taylor-Wood gave a sobering view of London life. Like a modern-day Hogarth she pictured an after-the-party scene, giving a high-class, high-pitched quality to domestic affairs within a narrative that even dedicated fans of soap opera would be hard put to follow. Finding a place in a well-known dramatic tradition, she transfused Joe Orton's comedy of manners and John Osborne's anger and watched as several sizzling strands of British culture came together in contemporary art.

The figure abounds, from Abigail Lane's sculpture of a half-naked man through to Ron Mueck, the Chapmans and Billingham. The approach is a mixture of the gothic and grotesque. Marc Quinn's chilled blood head stirred up an interest in returning to a classic genre of figuration and self-portraiture. Jenny Saville's figurative paintings bounced off her contemporaries. Embracing a set of traditional conventions, and rapidly achieving virtuosity, she transformed the ordinary through paint in works that are monumental in size and scale. Her suggestions of cosmetic surgery updated an art-historical discussion of the idealised nude seen from a feminist viewpoint. The conventions of painting flesh are overlaid with a contemporary anxiety and ambiguity akin to the work of Lucian Freud.

Damien Hirst shaped shared ideas and interests quickly and easily, his work developing during the decade to reflect changes in contemporary life. Relying on the straightforward appeal of colour and form, he made important art that contained little mystery in its construction. Adopting the graphic punch of billboard imagery, his work was arresting at a distance and physically surprising close up. Hirst understood art at its most simple and at its most complex. He reduced painting to its basic elements to eliminate abstraction's mystery. In the age of art as a commodity he made spot paintings – saucer-sized, coloured circles on a white ground – that became luxury designer goods. His art was direct but never empty. In the later spin paintings, which emphasised a renewed interest in a hands-on process of making, Hirst magnified a 'hobby'-art technique, drawing attention to the accidental and expressive energy of the haphazard. Influenced by Jeff Koons's basketballs floating in water (fig. 19), Hirst's early work used pharmacy medicine cabinets that showed the applied beauty of Modernist design. A cabinet of individual fish suspended in formaldehyde worked like the spot paintings, as an arrangement of colour, shape and form. This work came to be seen in the popular mind as a symbol of advanced art; overcoming an initial distrust of its ease of assembly, people became fascinated by how ordinary things of the world could be placed so as to be seen as beautiful. The work democratised its meaning, operating as simply as a pop song.

Hirst, understanding Collishaw's coup with the gunshot wound photograph, created work that brought together the joy of life and the inevitability

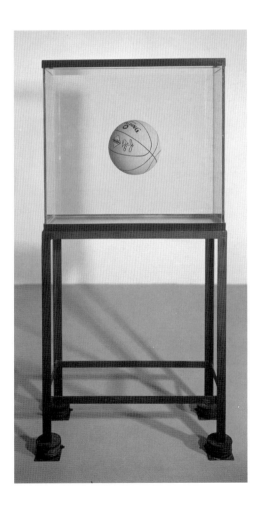

of death, in the process transforming the secrecy of Collishaw's voyeurism into mass spectacle. A scene of pastoral beauty became one of languid death: in *In and Out of Love*, newly emerged butterflies stuck to freshly painted monochromes; in *A Thousand Years* (p. 94), flies emerged from maggots, ate and died, zapped by an insect-o-cutor. Soon, the emphasis changed from an observation of creatures dying to the presentation of dead animals. A shark in a tank of formaldehyde presented a once life-threatening beast as a carcass: the glass box, half hunting trophy, half homage to the Minimalist object, imposed the gravity of a natural history museum onto an outsized council-house ornament. Hirst's sculpture progressed with the Arcadian beauty of a solitary sheep, *Away from the Flock* (p. 98), followed by the gothic thrill of the mechanically moving pig. Hirst understood the claustro-phobic horror of Francis Bacon's art (fig. 20), and found surprising parallels in the modern office or the lowly art tradition of portraits of animals. His fascination with the elevation of the commonplace, the unremarkable and the everyday has found Hirst at his most inventive.

The 'Sensation' exhibition is not the only possible picture of British art in the last decade. It is one man's view of how art has changed. But it substantially maps the contribution of those participants who have added to the diversity of what art is and what it can say. Each artist has contributed to the contemporary cultural debate, refining, expanding and developing the issues that new art always raises. Their work clearly reflects many of the concerns of British society, as well as touching plenty of raw spots on the national psyche. It has engaged and entertained an audience who find in it a reflection of their own pleasures, anxieties and phobias. A widely held suspicion of contemporary art is that it is a con, a hoax, and that the public must change its way of looking at art (and the world) if it is to understand it. This cynical speculation invariably resurrects the dreary question of longevity (and the implied warning against youth): 'Will it last 100 years?' This is unanswerable. The only guarantee is that its existing strengths and achievements will shape the art of tomorrow.

Fig. 20 **Francis Bacon**
Chimpanzee | 1955
Staatsgalerie Stuttgart, Germany
© Francis Bacon Estate

Thinking of You: An American's Growing, Imperfect Awareness

Brooks Adams

Since roughly 1990, Young British Art has been reaching American shores in ever quickening waves. Three broadly defined landing patterns may by now be discerned. First, that of the Artist Sprung Fully Formed: Damien Hirst, whose dramatic concepts and high-relief persona echoed the advent of Young American Art of the early '80s, or Rachel Whiteread, whose resonantly solemn casts of everyday structures and the spaces around them were instant classics. Next, there is the pattern of premature arrival, like the guest who shows up early and must incubate quietly, on the edges, while preparations continue: Gillian Wearing and Sam Taylor-Wood are good candidates for this role. Thirdly, come oscillating patterns of synergy, formed by energy fields emanating from both sides of the Atlantic, through which one may observe the progress over time of a traveller such as Gary Hume.

All in all, it seems that Young British Art has mostly arrived in this country in dribs and drabs – a 'serious' young painter here, a fresh rainmaker there, a few wallflowers hither and thither. (To this day, a few baby Brits have been examined here only through the pages of *Artforum*, *Frieze* and *Parkett*.) Not infrequently, work by a British tyro was trumpeted by vociferous word-of-mouth only to make its New York debut looking either half-baked or overcooked. Often enough, the artist would then disappear entirely from our view. Perhaps one went to London and saw something interesting – white architectural models, for instance, in 1992 at the Saatchi Gallery, by the team of Langlands & Bell – that wouldn't make it to New York for another five years. Occasionally, something or other young and British might be glimpsed by an American in Europe – in Germany at one of the recent Documentas (in '92 and '97), or in and around one of the last three Venice Biennales ('93, '95 and '97). Or an exceptionally large dose might have been swallowed all at once in Minneapolis in the fall of '95, when 'Brilliant! New Art from London' opened at the Walker Art Center. The non-Londoner's ability to travel fairly often and widely has proven to be an absolute must for keeping up with the Young British Art.

By the time work by Damien Hirst and Rachel Whiteread could be viewed here in New York in any kind of depth, both artists' reputations had long preceded them. We were hypnotised – amazed, up-in-arms, fascinated, threatened – by the flood of images of Hirst's encased shark, images that for several years here remained uncorroborated by any actual objects. The pickled predator remains the very symbol, and with hindsight the warning signal, for the invasion that ensued. Hirst may have been heralded in a timely enough manner, but in fact he did not have a major one-man exhibition in

New York until 1996, the year of his much-delayed inaugural at Gagosian. Thus, the surprise of that carnivalesque event was not only its scale but its unexpected variety: from sliced cows and mechanised pig, to Spin-Art paintings, to a giant ashtray full of butts – it had the crazed, cracked energy of a late-'70s Jonathan Borofsky extravaganza gone grizzly-gothic. Almost miraculously, given the US Customs' problems attending Hirst's taxidermical exercises – not to mention the then-fresh panic concerning British beef – the mood at the opening was cheerfully optimistic, indeed quite madly upbeat.

Whiteread's reputation had already achieved a sort of burnished moral glow in the infancy years of the chimeric invasion. A couple of years later – after the uproar in London over *House* (1993–4), but well before the artist revealed her plans for a Holocaust monument in Vienna – the glow had nearly completed its metamorphosis to halo. At the 1995 Carnegie International in Pittsburgh, there were signs of a backlash. Whiteread's *Untitled (One-Hundred Spaces)* (pp. 188–9) – a gorgeous, sensuous work consisting of 100 resin casts of the spaces under chairs, in the luminescent tones of half-sucked Life-Saver candies – was described in *The New York Times* as 'pretty', and lacking Bruce Nauman's grit. (Whiteread is often compared to Nauman, and the two artists are indeed inspired literalists in the way they both use non-*luxe* materials and direct sculptural casts. Some analogies, however, between Whiteread and a few of her closer contemporaries are also useful: to Robert Gober, for example, and *his* ghost objects of the late '80s and early '90s; to Guillermo Kuitca's global mattresses and plaintive apartment*werks*; to the monumental concrete poems of the architect Maya Lin.) The aura was restored when Whiteread, by now a venerable 33, was given her first, rather subdued one-woman show in New York in '96, at Luhring Augustine, in which she exhibited neoclassical waxen tubs worthy of Marat and bookshelf studies for the unrealised Vienna memorial.

On a number of occasions, American audiences have more simply been puzzled by the Young British Art. The show 'Brilliant!', for example, was perhaps not. Against the backdrop of foreboding cold of an early Midwestern winter, we were exposed to what seemed an almost unquantifiable number of emerging British artists, some as apparently interchangeable as the flakes lightly falling outside the museum. This was a veritable party of early arrivals. Quirky, self-consciously hapless videos and photo-documentations of mundane activities, gently skewed, were the order of the day. The show was notably short on Young British Artists who sculpt or paint: works by Hume, Whiteread, Glenn Brown and Alessandro Raho were somewhat perfunctorily included, but no Peter Doig or Fiona Rae. Nevertheless, glimmerings of promise were to be found. I clearly remember Gillian Wearing's *Dancing in Peckham* (1994), a colour videotape of the artist frugging with abandon, to the beat of her own different drummer, within the bustling precinct of an ordinary mall. Monadic as it was, it had a loopy presence, and it managed to conjure up a host of conflicting images: of Rita Tushingham in *A Taste of Honey* (1961) and Alicia Silverstone in *Clueless* (1995); of hard-

luck girls and Valley girls; of kitchen sinks vs. Range Rovers; of endurance art from the 1970s and 'pathetic' art of a few years ago.

Gary Hume has surely been the luckiest of Young British Artists. Not only did he come to our shores early and ready, but has ever since enjoyed the double good fortune of a successful gallery and prompt critical embrace. (Fiona Rae also showed up early and ready, in 1991, and attracted immediate interest. She was less lucky, however, when it came to dealers: she was given a first solo show in 1994 by John Good, who shortly thereafter closed his gallery's doors.) At Hume's initial show at Matthew Marks, in spring 1992, we got a first direct hit of his distinctive brand of hard-edged, Pop-inflected, quasi-absurdist neo-Minimalism: slickly rendered, high-gloss paintings in the campy colours of 'Mod' decors, that at first glance appear to be geometric abstractions, but turn out to be *portraits* of specific doors. Next, only months later, in a fall '92 group show at Barbara Gladstone curated by the British-born, New York-based Clarissa Dalrymple (a key conduit in all such youthful transatlantic matters), we were witness to what I think amounted to a out-and-out artistic crisis, perhaps caused by the unbearable stress of operating simultaneously as a very serious and ambitious painter, and as an equally serious, devil-may-care painter-prankster. But resolution and renewed vigour had evidently been attained by the fall of 1994. Hume, who had been living alternately in London and New York, showed a batch of tough, funny paintings that were more overtly figurative – sartorial accessories, silly figures and doggies had entered the picture – but that confirmed the artist's characteristic one-two punch of hot style and chill delivery. Most recently, in a yet bigger show in spring '97, he evoked a sultrier mood with a brooding palette of rich, dusky colours and figural elements – mystery bird silhouettes, a tentative tree – that suggested a departure into landscape. Hume's mercurial and visible progress has been at once enervating and exciting to behold.

Just as there are three transatlantic arrival patterns, so too has it become possible to detect (if only just) three dominant, frequently interwoven thematic strains within the new Young British Art. The first, largely indigenous to painting and three-dimensional-object making, indicates a Pop, Colour-Field, Mod or Techno influence and an attitude of imperturbable Kool (i.e. cool with a touch of toxic perversity). Hume and Hirst – also Mona

Fig. 21 Opposite • **Richard Smith**
Patty, Maxine, and Laverne | 1961
Collection of Richard L. Feigen, Chicago

Fig. 22 Above • **Alex Katz**
Winter Landscape | 1993
Saatchi Collection, London
© Alex Katz

Brooks Adams

Hatoum, Keith Coventry, Simon Callery, Richard Patterson and Gavin Turk – in their very different ways all show signs of this strain. In Hume's work, for instance, meet a number of well-defined lines connecting back to both the British Richard Smith (the cosmetics-hued semi-abstractions of the early-'60s; fig. 21), and the American Alex Katz (slick, pared-down landscapes and portraits; fig. 22). Through the devilish Hirst, Peter Greenaway and Jeff Koons get to indulge in a slow, metaphorical French kiss.

The second strain, more complex and more widely disseminated, might be called something like Post-Colonial Neo-Victorianism. Within this broad and aggressive theme, it is sometimes possible to detect an infrastructure of latter-day Minimalism (serial formats, 'systems' and the like) that harks back to the visual calendars and diaries of Peter Hutchinson or On Kawara, and especially Peter Greenaway's early films – beginning with the 'Alphabet' and 'Naming' pieces from the early '70s, on through *A Zed and Two Noughts* (1986, fig. 23), the tale of amputation-obsessed twin zoologist brothers, whose shared mistress is a murderous double-amputee.

This is fairly anxious material. And it is not, for the record, exclusively British: Alexis Rockman (fig. 24) is the outstanding specimen among young American artists working in this gothic-neurotic vein, painting beautifully executed, Old-Masterish allegories of sick minds and ecologies that suggest a synergistic rapport with the sci-fi, *vieux style* appropriations of the British painter Glenn Brown. While there is certainly a great deal of shape-shifting within the vast and motley array of Young British Artists, a significant number are pointedly and repeatedly drawn to projects requiring odd taxidermical skills and the iron stomach of a 19th-century naturalist or anatomical draughtsman. (Stubbs lives! Not least through the paintings of Mark Wallinger, whose *Race Class Sex* (pp. 178–9) of 1992 is the impeccable oil-portrait of four thoroughbred, bay-coloured horses.) Here again we find Hirst, of course, as well as Marc Quinn, whose perfectly academic self-portrait head is cast in his own, refrigerated blood. (He's nothing if not Kool.) But a work of the order of Abigail Lane's *Misfit* (1994, p. 111), the portrait-simulacrum of a poetically handsome young man, perhaps achieves something altogether more exalted, in giving new meaning and a third dimension to the notion of Pre-Raphaelite, Ruskinian verisimilitude.

But there are other Young British Artists (and young British writers, too, such as the deeply compelling Patrick McGrath) who have ventured way deeper into the realm of horror and the gothic-grotesque, Alain Miller and Paul Finnegan among them. But it is of course the Chapman brothers, Dinos and Jake, who most luridly spring to mind: their apocalyptic mutants might be the nuclear-age result of some long-forgotten meeting between the psychotically inspired Richard Dadd and John De Andrea's shock-of-the-real nudes of the '70s. The Chapmans are furthermore responsible for what may be the ultimate neo-Victorian monument to our times: *Ubermensch* (1995, p. 66), their outlandish tribute to Sir Stephen Hawking, portrayed in wheelchair, positioned on the top of a mountain in the manner of Sir Edwin Landseer's stag.

Not all Post-Colonial, Neo-Victorian Young British Artists sacrifice their own blood or lose their heads. Chris Ofili, for example, uses dreadlocked hair and elephant dung in his paintings and sculptures, which merely require collection visits to the local barber and zoo. Although Ofili did make a trip to Africa on a British Council grant (his original batch of elephant manure was indeed free-range), his rude objects – such as the self-explanatory, rolled *Shit Joint* of '95 – and painterly Afro-motifs primarily denote the often hallucinatory freedom of travel within the mind. For young British Post-Colonial artist-explorers like Ofili and Yinka Shonibare – who drapes mannequins in Victorian-style dresses made of contemporary African cloth – the generally local practice of collecting and shopping (today's gathering and hunting) has supplanted the Victorian field expedition to far-away lands.

The third strain is perhaps the most quintessentially home-grown, and seems to have descended more or less directly from Britain's own version of Arte Povera, the *circa* 1960 aesthetic of the Kitchen Sink. Hadrian Pigott, whose *Instrument of Hygiene (case 1)* (1994, p. 145) indicates Duchampian hybridisation (it is an actual sink-within-a-suitcase, complete with bars of soap) might be our poster boy. But the atmosphere of extreme, intensified and militant ordinariness – domestic difficulties and social trouble, everyday squalor and working-class grit – that defined the original Kitchen Sink aesthetic informs the production of many another Thatcher-era-educated Young British Artist. Richard Billingham's belligerently candid pictures of extraordinarily ordinary-seeming people-as-they-are, wherein 'warts' tend to eclipse all other features, are in fact part of an international movement in photography towards Kitchen-Sinkish *verité*, whether simulated or direct, whose participants range from Craigie Horsfield to Patrick Faigenbaum, and from Nan Goldin to Jeff Wall. Jenny Saville's Lucian-Freudian nude studies of women who live outside the standard boundaries of 'attractiveness' pack an unmistakable feminist punch. But once again it is the mercurial spirit of the effete Duchamp that lingers over work by both Whiteread and Sarah Lucas – tempered with the raunchier gut of the by now almost equally influential Nauman. Whiteread's elegant casts of the world-as-she-finds-it, along with Lucas's exuberantly inelegant ripostes – such as a fruit-and-vegetable sex-organ altar on a dirty mattress and the body-cast of a cigaretted sneer – together articulate the energy and span of Britain's Kitchen Sink aesthetic today.

The term itself, of course, immediately makes one think of British theatre and, especially, British cinema of the late '50s and early '60s. Over the last several months, I have been privy to a number of Delphic utterances on the part of Young British Artists, editors, critic-curators, and fledgling producers, to the effect that the next, burgeoning impulse of the Great British Zeitgeist will indeed emanate from a rebirth of avant-garde film. Recent work – film montages or filmic 'sculptures' – by the Glasgow-based Douglas Gordon lends credence to this notion. Congratulations to all concerned for his Turner Prize: America, these days, seems far less sure of its young artists.

Brooks Adams

Modern Medicis: Art Patronage in the Twentieth Century in Britain

Lisa Jardine

In May 1922 the Burlington Fine Arts Club in Savile Row, London, mounted a loan exhibition entitled 'The French School of the Last Hundred Years'.[1] Admission was by invitation only. Carefully assembled from the private collections of highly regarded contemporary art lovers, the Burlington exhibition made a firm statement against the conservatism of public gallery culture of the same period, particularly the National Gallery in London.[2] The anonymous reviewer in *The Connoisseur* was not impressed:

> Seurat's Landscape (lent by Mr Roger Fry) is an effort realistically to express the effect of a broad expanse of herbage seen under ordinary atmospheric conditions, but the result is an impression completely lacking in pictorial interest. The half-dozen works by Cézanne [lent by Gwendoline Davies and Maynard Keynes] make one wonder how this painter's great reputation has been achieved, since he neither attempted realism nor did he succeed in attaining a decorative effect. Daumier's *Head of a Man* (lent by Miss G. Davies) and *L'Avocat Triomphant* (lent by Mr William Burrell), display certainly, if somewhat too obviously, the technical abilities of their authors. In *l'Esprit Veille (Manaò Tupaù)*, (lent by Sir Michael and Lady Sadler), is given an example of Gauguin at his best – a best which is marred by the calculated *naïveté* of the presentation.[3]

The Impressionist and Post-Impressionist paintings exhibited had a decidedly more positive impact on the wealthy industrialist Samuel Courtauld. That September Courtauld bought his first Renoir. The following year he bought a second Renoir, two Gauguins, two Cézannes, two Manets, two Monets, a Daumier, a Seurat and a Van Gogh. The exhibition began his lifelong enthusiasm for the controversial work of Cézanne. He confided to Lydia Lopokova that he was 'jealous over' Keynes's Cézanne (fig. 27) which had been loaned to the Burlington exhibition, and that he 'used to admire even the photograph'.[4]

Samuel Courtauld's extraordinary gift of £50,000 to the British government a year later, to encourage the purchase of a collection of French Impressionist and Post-Impressionist paintings for the nation, ensured that his name and influence as a collector were permanently and publicly acknowledged. This makes him unusual – British collectors have tended characteristically to be more reticent and attention-shunning, probably to avoid the kind of snobbish disparagement with which conspicuous expenditure by the 'new rich' is traditionally treated in Britain.[5] But in every other respect the pattern of his encounter with, and subsequent passionate com-

Fig. 27 Above • **Paul Cézanne**
Still Life, Apples | *c.* 1879
By kind permission of King's College, Cambridge

Fig. 28 Opposite • **Edgar Degas**
La Répétition | *c.* 1877
The Burrell Collection, Glasgow

mitment as a collector of, avant-garde art of the moment is typical. He had a personal fortune at his disposal;[6] the work he first admired, fell in love with and desired, which formed the basis for his taste in art, belonged to other private collectors; that work was not the kind favoured by public art institutions, thus private rather than public gallery exhibitions shaped his buying strategies; once having been 'bitten' he purchased extravagantly, for pleasure, increasingly expertly, occasionally selling in order to finance further, better purchases.[7]

Courtauld's buying was clearly influenced by the opinions of those closely associated with the original 'French School of the Last Hundred Years' exhibition, and the 'Loan Exhibition of Modern Foreign Painting' at Colnaghi's Galleries in New Bond Street in 1924, organised by the Contemporary Art Society.[8] Among these were the artist and writer on contemporary art Roger Fry, the economist John Maynard Keynes, and Kenneth Clark, Keeper of Fine Art at the Ashmolean Museum in Oxford, and subsequently Director of the National Gallery. By the 1930s they and Courtauld frequented the same social circles, and he occasionally took their advice on a purchase.[9] None the less, Courtauld's most trusted advisor was always the dealer Percy Moore Turner, who ran the Independent Gallery, where Courtauld had purchased his first two Impressionist paintings in 1922.[10] When evaluating a potential purchase, an entrepreneurial businessman like Courtauld was looking for an assessment finely balanced between market value (a good price), quality as a work of art (in relation to strong emerging trends), and stature of the artist (now and in the future). Many major collectors have followed this practice of building a personal relationship with a commercial expert. One of Courtauld's contemporaries, the Scottish shipping magnate and renowned collector Sir William Burrell, expressed the view that 'a good dealer is more acute as a rule rather than a Professor. That is because the dealer if he makes a mistake has to pay.'[11]

William Burrell – a self-made industrialist – carried over his business astuteness into his art purchasing. His biographer characterises his activities as a connoisseur collector of a diverse range of art objects during the first 30 years of this century as follows: 'The amassing of a vast art collection was his great passion. In bringing together the Collection he applied the principles he had learned in the shipping world to the art market. He loved haggling and always kept a weather eye out for a bargain. He derived as much enjoyment from the pursuit of a work of art as he did from concluding a successful commercial transaction.'[12] Burrell himself tended to rely for purchasing advice on gallery owners David Croal Thompson and Alex Reid (though he resisted Reid's attempts to persuade him to buy *plein-air* Impressionists like Monet, Pissarro and Sisley, or the Post-Impressionists).[13] The pleasure he took in driving a hard bargain led him to steer clear of Joseph Duveen's gallery as 'too pricey'.[14]

The fact that Burrell eventually owned 22 paintings by Degas was due in no small part to the fact that Reid could assure him they were bargains. Between the wars Degas prices remained on the low side; Burrell's dearest

work, *La Répétition* (fig. 28), cost only £6,500 in 1926.[15] On the other hand, Burrell, like all passionate collectors, bought works by Degas because he loved them, and was driven almost obsessively to acquire them when they came on the market. In 1949 he wrote, 'I am sorry I never met Degas. Reid might have taken me to his studios had we been in Paris together but I was hardly ever in Paris at the same time as Reid.'[16]

The artists who made the work have always fascinated the collector. In the case of living artists, meeting them has often been only the beginning of the connoisseur's possible involvement.[17] Just before the First World War, Michael Sadler, Vice-Chancellor of Leeds University from 1911, bought a number of Kandinskys direct from the artist, after he had visited him in Germany. These featured prominently in his collection alongside work by Vanessa Bell, Roger Fry, Duncan Grant and Bernard Meninsky, and European Post-Impressionists, and substantially raised the profile of Kandinsky's work in this country.[18] The enthusiastic collector of contemporary English art, Edward Marsh, private secretary to Winston Churchill, met Mark Gertler, the Nash brothers and Stanley Spencer while they were still studying at the Slade, and became an assiduous backer of avant-garde English work. At various times both Gertler and Nash stayed in Marsh's London flat, and in November 1914 he offered to support Gertler to the tune of £10 a month for the duration of the war. Buying art by established artists, he decided, was too easy: 'How much more exciting to back what might roughly be called one's own judgement ... to go to the studios and the little galleries, and purchase, wet from the brush, the possible masterpieces of the possible Masters of the future.'[19] Here is another frequently repeated trait in private collectors of cutting-edge art – they like to be able to boast that they were the first to buy a particular young artist's work.[20]

Sir Kenneth Clark, one of the great British connoisseur collectors of the middle decades of this century, who assembled a remarkable collection of contemporary British art, regularly gave practical support to artists whose work he admired.[21] His personal patronage enabled Victor Pasmore (fig. 29), whom Clark considered 'one of the two or three most talented English painters of this century', to give up his job with the Greater London Council to paint full time.[22] Sustained and intermittent financial support, commitment to artists judged promising, commissioning and funding fabrication of new work – all of which characterised Clark's art-gathering activities – are typical of many patrons of new art. Clark later described the collection that resulted as 'a compromise between taste and opportunity ... it takes time to know what one really wants, and the process of discovering leaves one with a number of trial pieces.'[23]

Typically, 'new money' collectors have not limited their collecting to a single school, or even to art in one medium. The Robert and Lisa Sainsbury Collection at the University of East Anglia (given to the University in 1973) enshrines a characteristic 20th-century body of assorted art works originally assembled to grace the spacious family home of a notable entrepreneur. Now permanently displayed in a purpose-built gallery designed

by Sir Norman Foster and opened in 1978, the Sainsbury Collection contains both 20th-century art and art from Pre-Columbian America, the ancient Mediterranean civilisations, Africa, Oceania and Asia. The collection reflects the particular interests of its owners, with acquisitions clustered in areas of personal preference. Among the 20th-century works, the art of Henry Moore, Alberto Giacometti and Francis Bacon is particularly well represented (fig. 30).

Robert and Lisa Sainsbury 'found'[24] Francis Bacon in the '50s, bought his work at the modest prices it then commanded (£300 to £400), and got to know him personally.[25] In spite of his reputation for bad behaviour, Bacon apparently enjoyed being invited to their elegant social occasions.[26] The first portrait of a woman ever executed by Bacon (notoriously uninterested in the female form) was of Lisa Sainsbury. Over the years the couple acquired eleven major Bacon works, purchasing through the newly established London commercial galleries, the Hanover and the Marlborough.[27] Through their involvement with the Contemporary Art Society, which funded purchases in contemporary art for public galleries (including several Francis Bacons), they extended interest in the controversial artist's work to a wider audience. By the time their own collection became accessible to the general public Bacon was acknowledged as the leading British avant-garde artist, and his paintings were commanding six-figure sums.

Occasionally collectors are more single-mindedly driven by their passion. Ted Power, from the 1950s one of the great collectors of post-war international art in Britain, consistently pursued the most adventurous of avant-garde art purchases (for example, his early Kitajs, fig. 31).[28] Power, who had made his fortune in radio manufacture, 'bought with passion'. When he began to purchase Dubuffet in November 1955, the artist was barely known in England; Power bought over 80 works in the period 1955–60 alone.[29] The catalogue to an exhibition of some of Power's works (exhibited anonymously) in 1956 described him as a collector who 'buys new work while the paint is

Lisa Jardine

still wet, while the aesthetic with which to describe and evaluate it is still in the making … impulsively, experimentally, to see what will happen.'[30]

In general, the rule among 20th-century British collectors of art of all kinds has been, 'I buy because I love it' – anything from paintings to porcelain that takes the individual's fancy, and for which he or she has developed a keen sense of prevailing taste in the area, and purchasing expertise.[31] Describing works owned by him and shown at the Tate Gallery in 1952, Edward le Bas wrote: 'I have bought these paintings because I enjoy looking at them. Living in the day-to-day world, where one is constantly threatened by petty or temporal values, it is no small pleasure to have on the walls these various and complete visual worlds of shape and colour, each one made by the artist with thoughtful and emotional values that are both innocent and, I hope, enduring.'[32]

Does the act of purchasing itself contribute to a work's 'enduring' worth? In le Bas's formulation, the relationship between entrepreneurial purchasing acumen and 'taste' is typically unclear. How far are collectors with a reputation for having a 'good eye' or 'flawless taste' in fact being commended for their ability to establish a good competitive price for that kind of piece, at the same time as identifying its lasting aesthetic value and perhaps its relevance to an emerging school?[33]

Direct influence of wealthy private collectors over the formation of public taste becomes an issue when price and preference are brought into proximity with one another. A number of those who built up distinguished collections of modern art this century began their careers as dealers, or combined collecting with dealing. Most of those who bought art in quantity also sold, regularly returning work to the gallery of origin, and tending to sell as anonymously as possible.[34] Similarly, gallery owners frequently build up substantial, valuable collections of their own. Joseph Duveen, a highly respected dealer at the beginning of the century, was in a position at the end of his career to fund the Duveen Galleries for modern foreign art at the Tate Gallery.[35] Peggy Guggenheim, who opened her gallery of modern art in Cork Street in 1938, records that because 'it was extremely difficult to sell the work exhibited, I usually bought one painting or sculpture from each show in order to console the artist. Thus, without knowing it, I started my collection.'[36]

At a certain point, the art preferred by purchasers in the closely circumscribed world of private buyers and dealers percolates into the public domain. A number of significant collections this century have remained intact, either housed in their own gallery spaces (such as Courtauld's, Burrell's or the Sainsburys'), or bestowed whole or in part, as a gift or in lieu of death duties, to a major gallery (the Gwendoline Davies collection is now in the National Gallery of Wales; major works from Power's collection are in the Tate). They thereby inform the gallery-going public's taste in contemporary art alongside the art selected for the nation by the purchasing committee of the Arts Council and the directors and curators of our national public galleries.

Recently, collectors' treasures have become more rapidly visible to the public.[37] By the 1960s the nature of new art itself had a significant impact on the relationship between private collecting and public gallery spaces. Much of it was no longer wall-hung, and was too large and complicated for domestic-scale display.[38] The contractor Alistair McAlpine was a patron of New Generation sculpture in the late 1960s, but not many collectors had homes spacious enough to display work like Anthony Caro's (fig. 32).[39] The Saatchi Gallery in Boundary Road was started in 1985 and was a logical response to art that increasingly demanded to be displayed in rooms of warehouse scale, and which, indeed, frequently ironised its own relationship to such empty viewing spaces. The gallery dramatised the pivotal position of the late-20th-century art connoisseur, poised between the intimacy of his own enjoyment, and the public statements new art was trying to make.[40]

In the 1980s, new art moved strongly in the direction of theatrical interaction with its surroundings. Artists increasingly create environments that establish independent space to be entered by the viewer, rather than simply modifying the space given by the museum.[41] A sculptor like Richard Long, whose interventions can reasonably comfortably be accommodated to domestic interiors, is comparatively unusual, and predictably sought-after by private buyers (fig. 33). This kind of work has also proved attractive to collectors with access to corporate space (executive office suites, or gallery space alongside their head offices) in which to display it successfully.

At the end of the 20th century, gifts to the nation remain probably the most important intervention on the art scene by what is typically a reticent group, the major private patrons. Janet Wolfson de Botton's recent gift of 56 works by contemporary European and American artists from her personal collection for the new Bankside Tate Gallery was made in close consultation with the Tate's director, who was able to select work that strengthened and complemented the Tate's existing holdings in modern

Fig. 31 Left • **R.B. Kitaj**
The Murder of Rosa Luxemburg | 1960
The Tate Gallery, London
© R.B. Kitaj

Fig. 32 Above • **Anthony Caro**
Early One Morning | 1962
The Tate Gallery, London
© Anthony Caro

Fig. 33 Right • **Richard Long**
Slate Circle | 1979
The Tate Gallery, London
© Richard Long

Lisa Jardine

European art, thereby confirming its status as a 'historically responsible' gallery.[42] Andy Warhol's celebrated *Self-portrait* (1986), Gilbert and George's *Red Morning Trouble* (1977) (fig. 34), Bill Woodrow's *Elephant* (1984) and Cindy Sherman's series of *Film Stills* (1978–80) are particularly important additions. Her donations of work by Roni Horn, Gary Hume, Reinhard Mucha, Lucas Samaras and Nancy Spero will be the first examples of these artists to enter the Tate Collection.[43] So here is an alliance between collector and director of a major collection, collaborating to establish a recognisable tradition, and to enlarge the horizons of contemporary art in Britain.

The interactions between patrons, dealers and artists have always been complicated and their relationships often strained. There is inevitably a temptation, looking at the ferment that is the contemporary scene in Young British Art, to believe that disorder is, as it were, the order of the day.[44] But it was ever thus. In spite of sometimes insistent claims that new art collecting today has degenerated into something close to banking, or speculating in futures, the contours of purchase made and pleasure sought have remained throughout the 20th century startlingly similar to their origins in the High Renaissance.[45] 'Collectors are selfish heroes', as one dealer told me.[46] In pursuit of their own private passions, the money they spend and the work they acquire are linked in a virtuoso on-going process – bravely taken decisions for personal gratification, whose outcome is a 'tradition', however bizarrely shaped.

When, in 1502, Isabella d'Este asked Francesco Malatesta in Florence to approach the painter Perugino on her behalf, Malatesta advised against the project. Perugino, he told Isabella, was a difficult man to deal with, and he suggested employing more reliable 'great names', like Filippino Lippi or Sandro Botticelli instead. She was determined, persisted and the artist eventually agreed, though he was outrageously late delivering the finished painting (the price was an irresistible 100 ducats, twenty of which were paid in advance). Perugino's *Triumph of Chastity* thereby took its place in the Renaissance artistic tradition we continue to recognise today.[47] Fifty years from now we will probably have no greater trouble identifying the line of development of Young British Art, from its roots in Bacon and Caro to the end of the 20th century, and, as always, we will conveniently have forgotten the crucial role within it played by vigorously entrepreneurial collectors.[48]

Fig. 34 **Gilbert and George Red Morning Trouble** | 1977

I would like to express my gratitude to Kate Bingham, who helped me with the research for this essay. A number of people were kind enough to provide me with background (in person or on paper) on the contemporary collecting scene, including Edward Lee, Nicholas Logsdail and Nicholas Serota. The following publications and organisations generously helped me with cuttings and literature: *Art Monthly, Art Newspaper, Modern Painters, Frieze,* Starkmann Limited, Tate Gallery, White Cube, *Vogue.*

Lisa Jardine

1. John House, 'Modern French art for the nation: Samuel Courtauld's collection and patronage in context', in John House (ed.), *Impressionism for England: Samuel Courtauld as Patron and Collector*, exh. cat., London, 1994, pp. 9–34.

2. The Tate Gallery had refused Gwendoline Davies's offer to lend two of her Cézannes in 1921, and had twice turned down a loan of Sir Hugh Lane's collection of Impressionist paintings. (House, *Impressionism for England*, pp. 10–13).

3. 'Burlington Fine Arts Club', *The Connoisseur*, 63, July 1922, pp. 177–8, reprinted House, *Impressionism for England*, p. 238.

4. Polly Hill and Richard Keynes (eds), *Lydia and Maynard: Letters between Lydia Lopokova and John Maynard Keynes*, London, 1989, p. 260; cit. House, *Impressionism for England*, p. 12.

5. Keynes confided to Lydia Lopokova that Courtauld's gift to the nation smacked of social advancement and was 'aimed at a peerage' (in 1937 Courtauld declined a peerage). See House, *Impressionism for England*, p. 28.

6. For an interesting graph of Courtauld's company income against his expenditure on art see 'The Courtauld family and its money 1594–1947', in House, *Impressionism for England*, p. 54.

7. All these traits can be paralleled in the building of collections of Young British Art by 1980s and '90s collectors. The Courtauld Trust agreement contained a clause stating that pictures purchased could be resold and the money spent on upgrading the collection, thereby ackowledging Courtauld's own practice as a private collector. Normally, public institutions have no such freedom to discard or 'upgrade'.

8. The Contemporary Art Society had been formed to purchase and exhibit modern European art in 1909. Alan Bowness *et. al.*, *British Contemporary Art 1910–1990: Eighty Years of Collecting by The Contemporary Art Society*, London, 1991.

9. In 1929 Fry urged Courtauld to buy a Gauguin and a Cézanne. Letters from Fry to Courtauld, 22 and 28 March, 31 July 1929 (Courtauld Institute Archives).

10. House, *Impressionism for England*, p. 22. Turner frequently travelled abroad to investigate pictures on Courtauld's behalf, both for his private collection and for the Courtauld Trust.

11. Richard Marks, *Burrell: A Portrait of a Collector: Sir William Burrell 1861–1958*, Glasgow, 1983, p. 118.

12. Ibid., pp. 18–19.

13. Ibid., pp. 20–1.

14. Ibid., p. 130.

15. Ibid., p. 121. Peak periods for art-purchasing this century have followed collapses in prices – the Depression, the immediate post-war periods. The current flurry of purchasing in the late 1990s follows seven or so years of depressed prices in the commercial galleries.

16. Ibid.

17. It has proved easier to research major collections assembled by male collectors. Many of them collected collaboratively with their wives (Courtauld stopped collecting altogether on his wife's death). Given the reticence of most British art collectors, more research is needed into the significant number of distinguished women collectors, from Sickert's ex-wife Ellen Cobden-Sanderson and Gwendoline Davies to the present day.

18. *British Contemporary Art*, p. 27

19. Ibid., pp. 28–9.

20. Contemporary dealers tell me that prominent collectors (in Britain and abroad) of Young British Art like to 'find' new talent before it is ever offered commercial gallery space.

21. For the range of Clark's collection see Sotheby's London catalogue, June 1984, *Paintings and Works of Art from the Collections of the late Lord Clark of Saltwood OM, CH, RCB*. He also gave advice on purchasing to other wealthy collectors. Clark and Sir Jasper Ridley advised Queen Elizabeth the Queen Mother in her modern art buying. See John Cornforth, *Queen Elizabeth the Queen Mother at Clarence House*, London, 1996, pp. 31–3. A lot more could be said about this kind of 'word of mouth' influence of one private art collector on others. New art is admired in one collector's home, then sought out in the galleries and purchased.

22. Kenneth Clark, *Another Part of the Wood*, London, 1974, p. 251.

23. *Seventeen Collectors: An Exhibition of Paintings and Sculpture*, exh. cat., London, Tate Gallery, 1952; cit. *British Contemporary Art*, p. 73.

24. '[Sidney Nolan] whom I had found (not "discovered") twenty years before had grown to be a great name in modern art' (Kenneth Clark, *The Other Half*, London, 1977, p. 195).

25. Colin Anderson first drew Robert Sainsbury's attention to Bacon's work (Anderson was responsible for the purchase of Bacon's *Figure Study II* for the CAS in 1946).

26. Michael Peppiatt, *Francis Bacon: Anatomy of an Enigma*, London, 1996, pp. 166–7.

27. The Marlborough Gallery started the practice of paying significant artists on its list a salary, thus drawing talent away from competitors. Financial support for new talent – salaries, fabrication costs for new work, production costs for a catalogue, or an expensive one-man show – is still one of the ways commercial galleries affect the fortunes of artists in the 1990s. Michael Craig-Martin records that in the early days of his career, the dealer Jay Jopling (now

of White Cube) was crucial to him: 'When Damien had a mad idea that was ridiculously expensive to realise, Jay would simply go about getting the money so that it could be done, rather than figure out how to do it on the cheap' (Louisa Buck, *GQ*, February 1995).

28. Power bought four of his earliest paintings in 1952 from Arthur Tooth & Sons' gallery in London. Peter Cochrane of Tooth's became a lifelong friend, and played an important role in helping him build up his collection, while another partner, David Gibbs, often bought with Power in mind. Jennifer Mundy, 'The challenge of post-war art: the collection of Ted Power', in Jennifer Mundy (ed.), *Brancusi to Beuys: Works from the Ted Power Collection*, London, 1996, p. 12.

29. Mundy, *Brancusi to Beuys*, p. 10. The first Dubuffet show in England was at the ICA in March 1955, and was virtually ignored by the critics (ibid., p. 13). Like most large-scale collectors, Power regularly sold work, sometimes in quantity, to release funds to buy new work, or to 'upgrade' his existing holdings.

30. Lawrence Alloway, 'Introduction: the challenge of post-war painting', *New Trends in Painting: Some Pictures from a Private Collection*, exh. cat., Arts Council, 1956–7, p. 5.

31. Every contemporary collector I spoke to as part of the research for this essay told me 'Collecting is a passion close to obsession', and 'I buy a work simply because I love it'. The dealer Jay Jopling (who once sold fire extinguishers as a holiday job) explained, 'Art is different. Collectors fall in love with things. It's difficult to fall in love with a fire extinguisher.' (*Dazed and Confused*, 5, n.d.)

32. *British Contemporary Art 1910–1990*, p. 72

33. '[Kenneth Clark's] private collection was not the collection of an aggregator; it was the collection of someone who loved art' (John Pope-Hennessy, *Learning to Look*, London, 1991, pp. 299–300).

34. All the work on early collectors I have looked at indicates that identifying what a collector sold and when has proved extremely difficult. Those contemporary collectors I consulted indicated that the strategy of discreet resale through the gallery of origin continues today.

35. House, *Impressionism for England*, p. 11.

36. Peggy Guggenheim, 'Introduction' to *The Peggy Guggenheim Collection*, exh. cat., London, Tate Gallery, 1964–5. During the early years her exhibitions included Kandinsky, Tanguy, John Tunnard, Henry Moore, Calder, Duchamp-Villon, Brancusi, Arp and his wife Taeuber-Arp, Max Ernst, Picasso, Braque and Schwitters.

37. The trend for private purchasers immediately to loan large-scale works to public galleries is more marked in the United States. On the relationship between American private collectors and gallery spaces see Lisa Jardine, 'Art and money: SFMOMA', *Modern Painters*, Spring 1997, pp. 84–7.

38. On the changing role of the museums of modern art in public taste formation see most recently Nicholas Serota, *Experience or Interpretation: The Dilemma of Museums of Modern Art*, London, 1996. A number of distinguished private collectors have also served on the buying committees of the Contemporary Art Society and Patrons of New Art at the Tate Gallery, and on the judging panel for the Turner Prize, thereby once again enabling private connoisseurship to influence public awareness of particular art and artists.

39. 1990s dealers I spoke to acknowledged that Young British Art too tended to need museum-sized spaces, and special installation.

40. See Lisa Jardine, 'Fiona Rae and Gary Hume at the Saatchi Gallery', *New Statesman*, 10 January 1997, pp. 38–9.

41. See Serota, *Experience or Interpretation*, pp. 27–36.

42. Contemporary gallery owners tend to make a distinction between such responsible collections, which allow the novice to understand the historical process to which new art belongs, and a kind of 'instant gratification' model, which seeks for impact and thrill, with no further justification beyond immediate consumerist pleasure.

43. Press release, Tate Gallery, 3 October 1996.

44. There is, in any case, a strong desire on the part of those involved in the art scene to romanticise it as disorderly. See most recently, Matthew Collings, *Blimey! From Bohemia to Britpop: The London Artworld from Francis Bacon to Damien Hirst*, Cambridge, 1997.

45. For a fuller version of this argument see L. Jardine, *Worldly Goods: A New History of the Renaissance*, London, 1996.

46. Nicholas Logsdail of the Lisson Gallery, personal communication, May 1997.

47. Julia Cartwright, *Isabella d'Este Marchioness of Mantua 1474–1539*, 2 vols, London, 1903.

48. It is striking that Jay Jopling, the leading younger dealer in the British art market, acknowledges the roots of his own artistic formation as originating with Bacon and Caro. It was his 'teenage passion for the fleshy existential paintings of Francis Bacon' at the Tate which first triggered his artistic awareness at fourteen (Louisa Buck, *GQ*, February 1995). For his first charity sale in 1986 he rejected an Anthony Caro drawing, visited the artist, and brazenly requested a sculpture (it made £15,000).

Darren Almond

Richard Billingham

Glenn Brown

Simon Callery

Jake & Dinos Chapman

Adam Chodzko

Mat Collishaw

Keith Coventry

Peter Davies

Tracey Emin

Paul Finnegan

Mark Francis

Alex Hartley

Marcus Harvey

Mona Hatoum

Damien Hirst

Gary Hume

Michael Landy

Abigail Lane

Langlands & Bell

Sarah Lucas

Martin Maloney

Jason Martin

Alain Miller

Ron Mueck

Chris Ofili

Jonathan Parsons

Richard Patterson

Simon Patterson

Hadrian Pigott

Marc Quinn

Fiona Rae

James Rielly

Jenny Saville

Yinka Shonibare

Jane Simpson

Sam Taylor-Wood

Gavin Turk

Mark Wallinger

Gillian Wearing

Rachel Whiteread

Cerith Wyn Evans

Darren Almond

A Bigger Clock | 1997 | steel, perspex, aluminium, paint, motor, 154 x 206 x 98 cm

Richard Billingham

Untitled | 1993–5 | colour photographs on aluminium, varied measurements (pages 53–7)

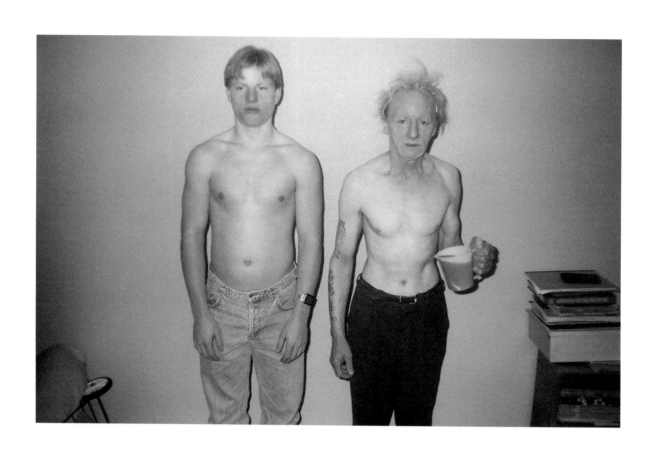

Richard Billingham

Richard Billingham

Glenn Brown

The Day the World Turned Auerbach | 1992 | oil on canvas, 56 x 50.5 cm

Dali-Christ | 1992 | oil on canvas, 274 x 183 cm

Glenn Brown

60

Ornamental Despair (Painting for Ian Curtis) After Chris Foss | 1994 | oil on canvas, 201 x 300 cm

Glenn Brown

Simon Callery

Newton's Note | 1996 | oil on canvas, 255 x 320 cm

Jake & Dinos Chapman

Great Deeds Against the Dead | 1994 | mixed media with plinth, total 277 x 244 x 152 cm

Ubermensch | 1995 | fibreglass, resin, paint, 366 x 183 x 183 cm

Jake & Dinos Chapman

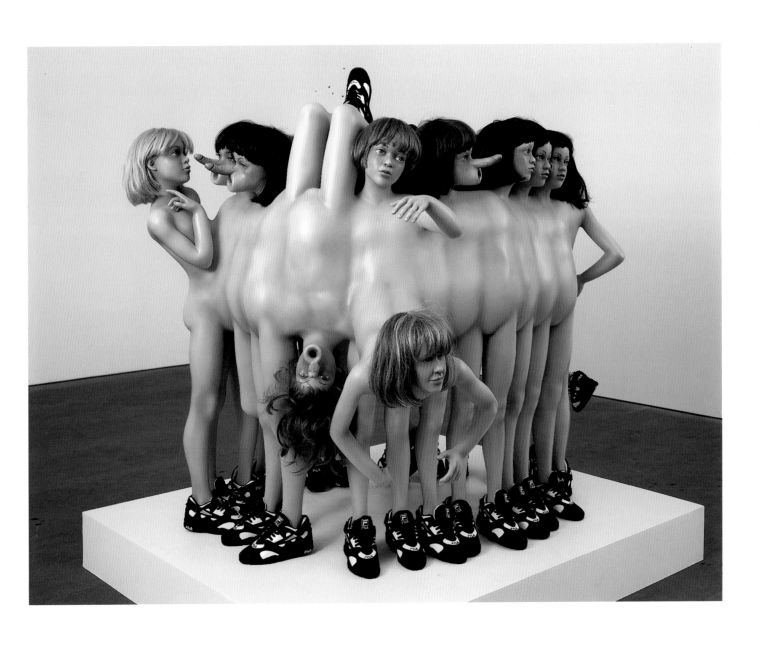

Zygotic acceleration, biogenetic, de-sublimated libidinal model (enlarged x 1000) | 1995
fibreglass, 150 x 180 x 140 cm, plinth 180 x 20 x 150 cm

Jake & Dinos Chapman

Tragic Anatomies | 1996 | fibreglass, resin, paint, smoke devices, varied measurements

Jake & Dinos Chapman

69

Adam Chodzko

The God Look-Alike Contest | 1992–3
(Last Judgement Version)
mixed media, each 57 x 44.5 x 2.5 cm

Mat Collishaw

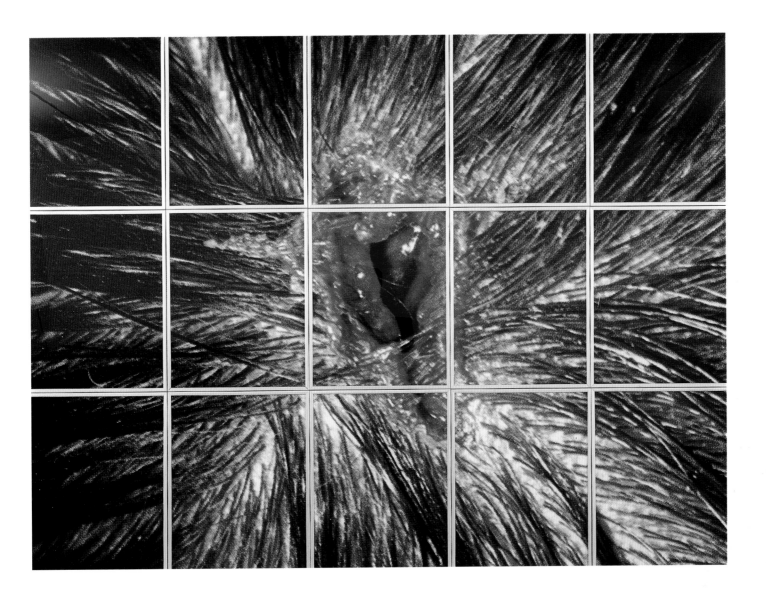

Bullet Hole | 1988–93 | cibachrome mounted on 15 light boxes, 229 x 310 cm

Keith Coventry

White Abstract (Sir Norman Reid Explaining Modern Art to the Queen) | 1994 | oil on canvas, wood, gesso, glass, 66 x 105 x 7.2 cm

Peter Davies

Art I like is Sean Landers the most important artist of his generation, Bruce Nauman all that aggressive white male rage stuff, Mike Kelley he does everything so trashy but we love it, Damien Hirst he knows how to state the obvious big time with such panache, Jean Michel Basquiat wah wah stylee Jimi Hendrix air guitar, Willem de Kooning like you spilt all your nursery school colours and swilled them around beautiful, Cy Twombly then you scribbled on the black board when the teachers not looking + tried to rub it out, Picasso he just did whatever the fuck he wanted, Fiona Rae she puts it all together, Bridget Riley so complicated but such eloquent funky results, Julian Schnabel total audacious aggression yes please, Rachel Whiteread in contrast such tranquility and grace but tuff enuff, Donald Judd wanted to take over the world don't we all, Peter Halley just what is he wittling on about maybe he feels imprisoned or something, Caroll Dunham what a dude! can't believe those things actually exist they mean so much to me, Brice Marden scary monster, Gerhard Richter the day of the living dead, Signar Polke super trooper up yours he's in total control, Joseph Beuys just drop some acid and I'll take his word for it more like Bugs Bunny, Agnes Martin now that is total terror vision and its deserts too, Gary Hume now that's for dessert blancmange meets Haagen-Daz, Jason Fox megaphone drone he's been reading Fat Freddy's Kat, Alex Katz its kind of timeless but oh those night scenes, Luc Tuymans now I wouldn't like to meet him down a dark alley, Peter Doig elesse super cool the loneliness of a downhill racer, Glen Brown oh when the saints come marching in repro classics, Sarah Lucas her hard hitting empowerment attitude, Louise Bourgeois tough tits she'll rip you to bits, Bernard Cohen kind of all the fun of the fair, Karen Kilimnik after dark sheer black magic, Lily Van der Stoker Mutha Fucka, John Baldessari that hand painting stuff and also that writing he's like Bruce Springsteen - the boss, Gilbert + George now people say they're kind of risqué but they're so sincere, Antony Caro now he really is one mean badass M.F.s oB, Velasquez he's Versace for art lovers, Turner he's like some Byron/Shelley opium high, Sherrie Levine now that's got to be tongue in cheek how else could anyone be bothered to do that shit, Andy Warhol my fucking headmaster now was he trying to set an example or what, Josef Albers totally up to date if you want the funkest thing hardei could get their hands on today check this out, Richard Prince now this really is the greatest thing if ever there was dare faced cheek it would be in this spirit (see the Blue Lagoon), Meg Cranston L.A. style funk + sexiness only with the brains attached, Richard Patterson broom broom, Matisse he had no problems with some fucker telling him his work looked decorative, Pissarro logical progression but Is yt is gay is totally radical, Jenny Holzer she's gotta be like one of those stand up comedians who always manages to keep a straight face + does loads of charity work, Charles Ray he's like a fucking spoilt brat with this giant dolls + trucks + Run DMC style hat and sneakers, John Currin now if ever anyone turned a love for Metallica to their advantage, Paul McArthy guess he never saw Tiswas but he must've seen Texas Chainsaw whilst eating a McDonalds (hello Ronald), David Salle he's kind of Tom Jones of the art world but I dug that stuff it was really clever, Ellsworth Kelly his work is just so wonderful it leaves me speechless but then I always liked kites, William Tucker "Maybe when your life is close at hand, maybe then you'll understand" Now that's what I call music, Kiki Smith (Iron Maiden), Dave Hammons Yardbird suite aint that neat, Ashley Bickerton word up Cameo meets Ray Petri, Michael Craig Martin you know immediately what he's on about, Richard Deacon another space case trip indulger, Max Beckmann hey you the rock steady crew, Larry Clark now that's what I call stream of consciousness don't give a damn excitement, Jeff Wall he's got an eye for detail look at those fashion statements slyly disguised as history paintings, Dan Graham spiel spiel house + gardens meets Lawnmower man, Barnett Newman tranquility, Frank Stella it's acid House, Constable total memorabilia, Juan Miro kind of art director over design, designs, Tatlin a complete + utter Fruit + nutcase, Aleksandr Rodchenko kind of taste ful rug Star wars, Beat Streuli kind of Malevich cool but kind of limited, El Lissitsky cool got better angles more Star wars, d'ya think he'd hang with Schnabel Pervie, Bill Viola total smart Arse - gotta hand it to him, Oskar Kokoshka a bit of an alien life form, in another life, Vincent Van Gogh young Soul rebel, Claes Oldenburg combine harvester the wicked witch of the West Carl Jasper Johns wins thru on its seductiveness, Mitja Tusek kind of downright groovy, Chris Burden black humour, Vito Acconi Ostend up don't be fooled a total traditionalist, Kenny Scharf adolescent sniggering meets P funk, Andreas Gursky kind of naughty boy sent to corner of classroom, Christian Schumann left over 60's hippy sentiments with 90's technology, Giuseppe absurd qualities, Thomas Struth taught art, Bernard Frize left over 60's hippy sentiments, Meyer Vaisman fake animals, Christoph Penone lack of vision, Jannis Kounellis live animals, Thomas Grunfeld dead animals, Meyer Vaisman fake animals, Christoph Wool if you can't take a joke get the fuck out of my house, Phillip Taaffe control freak, Marina Abramovic

Text Painting | 1996 | acrylic on canvas, 203 x 254 cm

Everyone I Have Ever Slept With 1963–1995
1995 | appliquéd tent, mattress, light
122 x 245 x 214 cm

Paul Finnegan

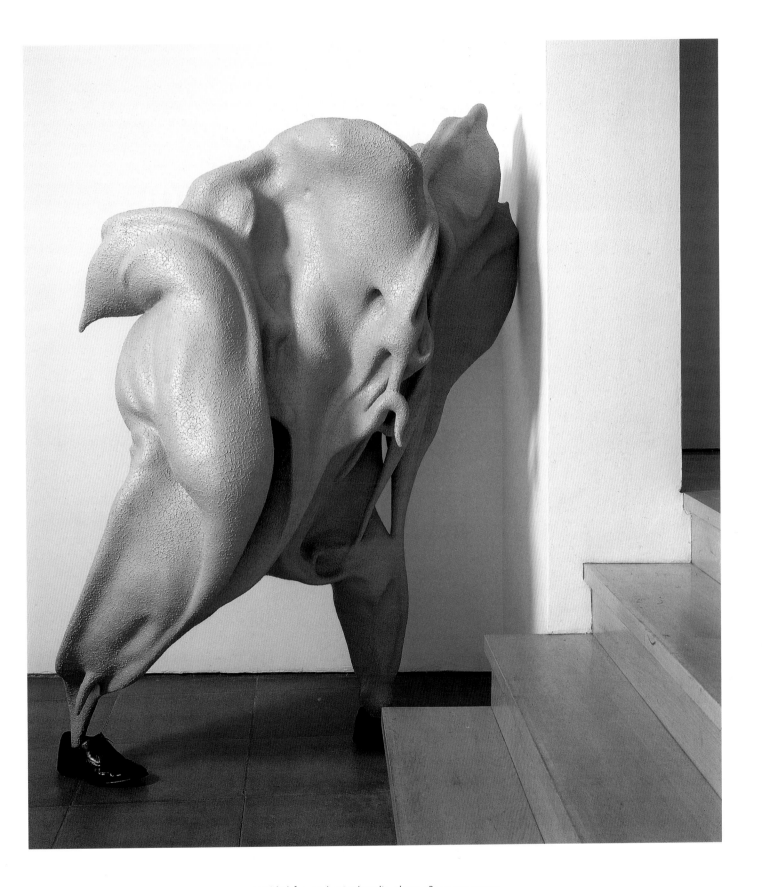

Untitled | 1995 | mixed media, shoes, 185 x 140 x 90 cm

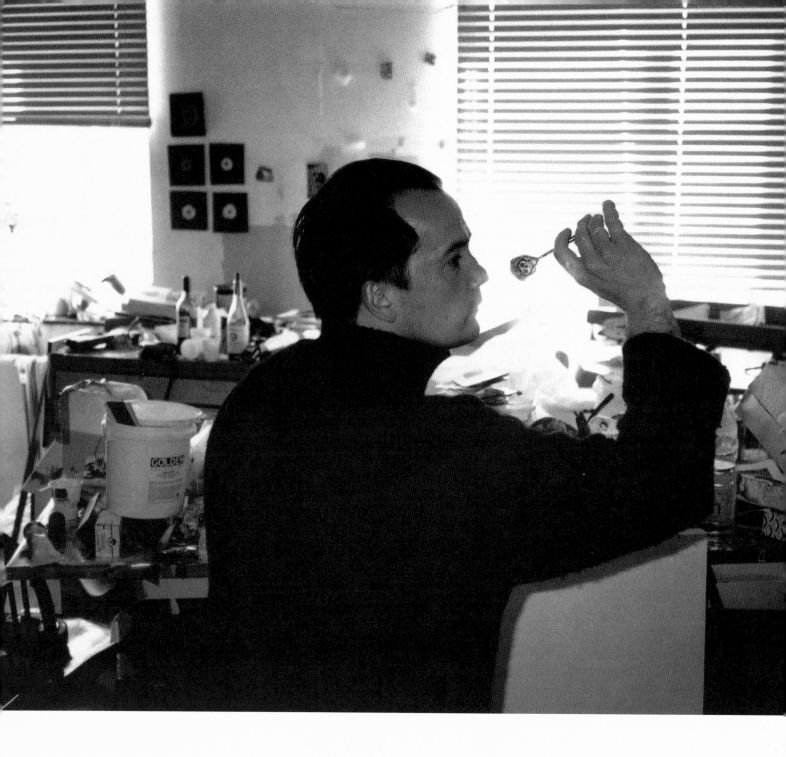

Mark Francis

Negative | 1995 | oil on canvas, 244 x 214 cm

Alex Hartley

Untitled (Ronan Point) | 1995 | black-and-white photograph, MDF, steel, 200 x 90 x 35 cm

Marcus Harvey

Myra | 1995 | acrylic on canvas, 396 x 320 cm

Proud of His Wife | 1994 | oil and acrylic on canvas, 198 x 198 cm

Marcus Harvey

Dudley, Like What You See? Then Call Me | 1996 | acrylic on canvas, 198 x 198 cm

Marcus Harvey

Mona Hatoum

Deep Throat | 1996 | table, chair, television set, glass plate, fork, knife, water glass, laser disc, laser disc player
74.5 x 85 x 85 cm

Damien Hirst

The Physical Impossibility of Death in the Mind of Someone Living | 1991
tiger shark, glass, steel, 5% formaldehyde solution, 213 x 518 x 213 cm

Damien Hirst

94

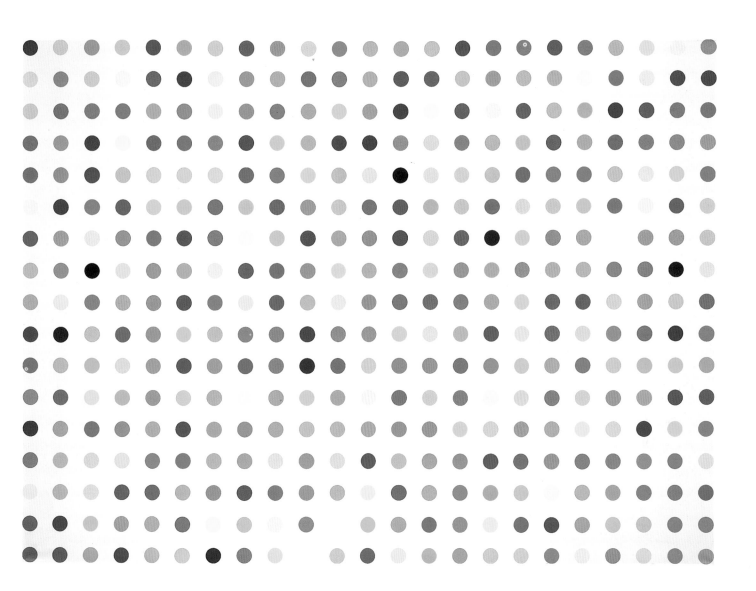

Above · **Argininosuccinic Acid** | 1995 | gloss household paint on canvas, 335 x 457.2 cm
Opposite Above · **Isolated Elements Swimming in the Same Direction for the Purpose of Understanding** | 1991
MDF, melamine, wood, steel, glass, perspex cases, fish, 5% formaldehyde solution, 183 x 274 x 30.5 cm
Opposite Below · **A Thousand Years** | 1990 | steel, glass, flies, maggots, MDF, insect-o-cutor, cow's head, sugar, water, 213 x 427 x 213 cm

Damien Hirst

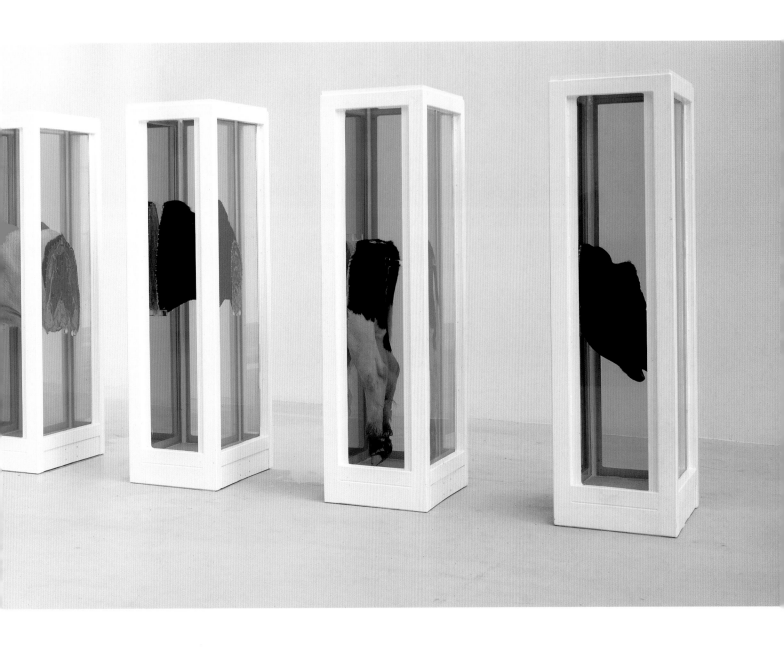

Some Comfort Gained from the Acceptance of the Inherent Lies in Everything | 1996
steel, glass, cows, formaldehyde solution, 12 tanks, each 200 x 90 x 30 cm

Damien Hirst

Away from the Flock | 1994 | steel, glass, lamb, formaldehyde solution, 96 x 149 x 51 cm
This little piggy went to market, this little piggy stayed at home | 1996 | steel, GRP composites, glass, pig, formaldehyde solution, electric motor
2 tanks, each 120 x 210 x 60 cm

Damien Hirst

98

beautiful, kiss my fucking ass painting | 1996 | gloss household paint on canvas, diameter 213.4 cm

Damien Hirst

Gary Hume

Begging For It | 1994 | gloss paint on panel, 200 x 150 cm

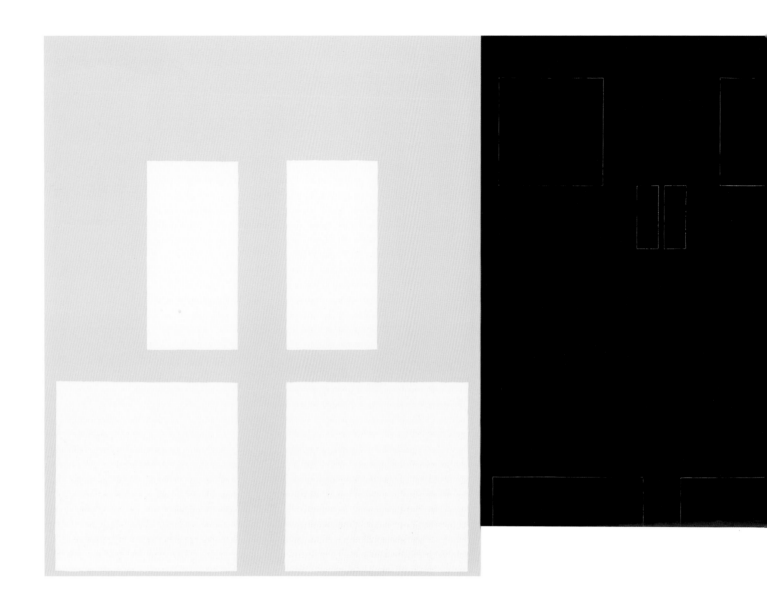

Dolphin Painting No IV | 1991 | gloss paint on MDF board, 4 panels, total 222 x 643 cm

Gary Hume

103

Tony Blackburn | 1994 | gloss paint on panel, 194 x 137 cm

Gary Hume

Vicious | 1994 | gloss paint on panel, 218 x 181 cm

Gary Hume

My Aunt and I Agree | 1995 | gloss paint on aluminium panel, 200 x 1100 cm

Gary Hume

Michael Landy

Costermonger's Stall | 1992–7 | wood, gloss paint, tarpaulin, plastic buckets, electric lights, flowers, 182.8 x 213.3 x 213.3 cm

Abigail Lane

Misfit | 1994 | wax, plaster, oil paint, human hair, clothing, glass eyes, 60 x 85 x 192 cm

Langlands & Bell

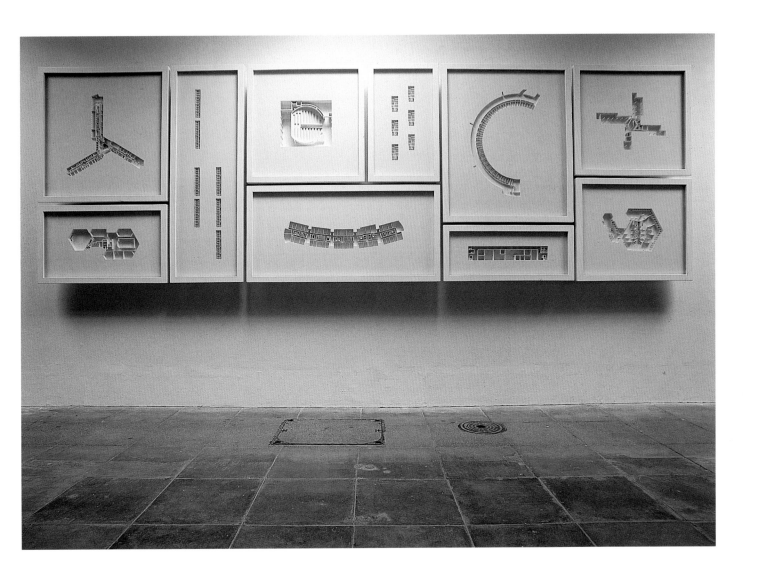

Ivrea | 1991 | hardwood, wood products, glass, cellulose lacquer, total 160 x 500 x 18 cm

Sarah Lucas

Au Naturel | 1994 | mattress, water bucket, melons, oranges, cucumber, 83.8 x 167.6 x 144.8 cm

Two Fried Eggs and a Kebab | 1992 | photograph, fried eggs, kebab, table, 76.2 x 152.4 x 89 cm

Sarah Lucas

Above Left · **Figleaf in the Ointment** | 1991
plaster, hair, lifesize
Above Centre · **Receptacle of Lurid Things** | 1991
wax, lifesize
Above Right · **1 – 123 – 123 – 12 – 12** | 1991
size seven boots with razor blades

Right · **Where Does it All End?** | 1994–5
wax and cigarette butt, 6.4 x 9.5 x 6.4 cm

Sarah Lucas

Sod You Gits | 1990 | photocopy on paper, 216 x 315 cm

Sarah Lucas

Bunny | 1997 | tights, plywood chair, clamp, kapok stuffing with wire, 101.5 x 90 x 63.5 cm

Sarah Lucas

Martin Maloney

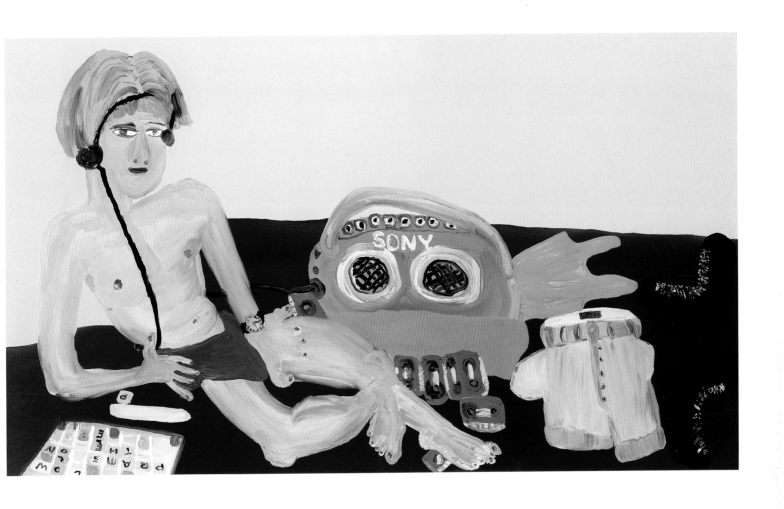

Sony Levi | 1997 | oil on canvas, 173.5 x 298 cm

Jason Martin

Merlin | 1996 | oil on aluminium, 244 x 244 cm

Alain Miller

Eye Love Eye | 1997 | oil on canvas, 235 x 195 cm

Ron Mueck

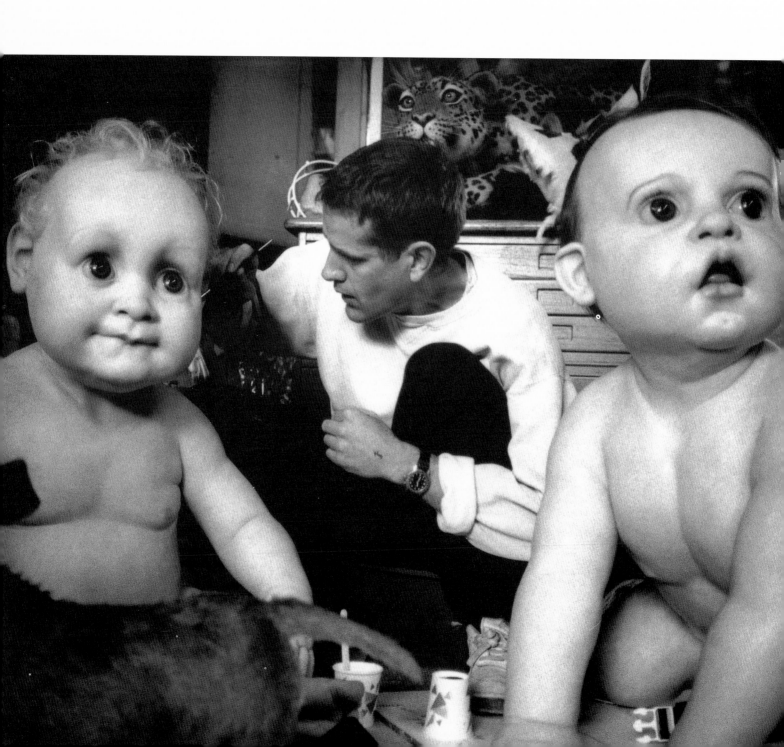

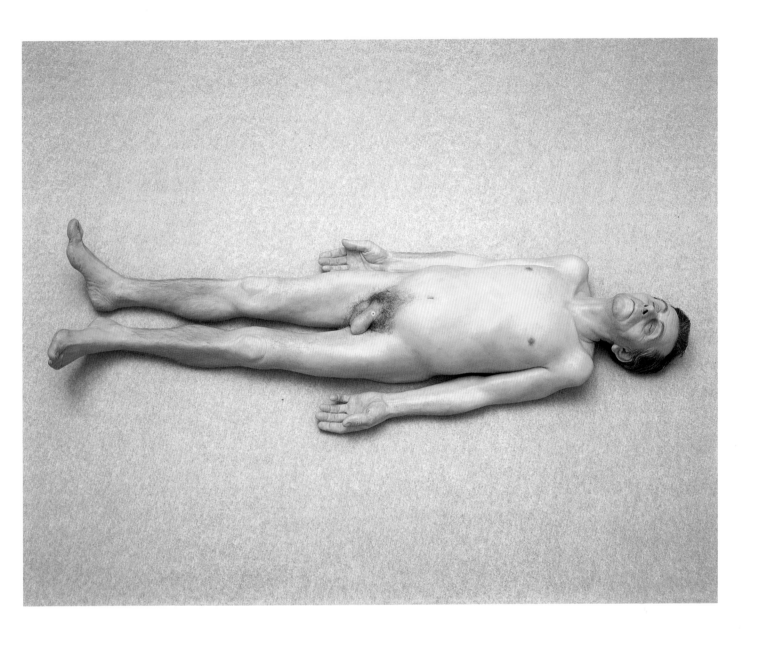

Dead Dad | 1996–7 | silicone and acrylic, 20 x 102 x 38 cm

Chris Ofili

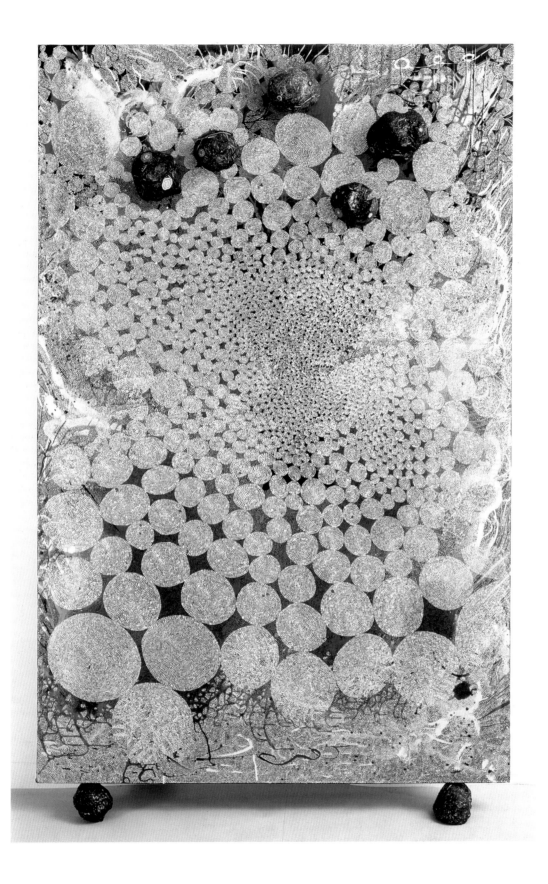

Spaceshit | 1995 | oil paint, polyester resin, map pins, elephant dung on linen, 183 x 122 cm

Afrodizzia | 1996 | paper collage, oil paint, glitter, polyester resin, map pins, elephant dung on linen, 243.8 x 182.9 cm

Chris Ofili

130

Popcorn Tits | 1996 | oil paint, paper collage, glitter, polyester resin, map pins, elephant dung on linen, 183 x 122 cm

Chris Ofili

131

Afrobluff | 1996 | acrylic paint, oil paint, paper collage, polyester resin, map pins, elephant dung on linen, 243.8 x 182.9 cm

Chris Ofili

The Holy Virgin Mary | 1996 | paper collage, oil paint, glitter, polyester resin, map pins, elephant dung on linen, 243.8 x 182.9 cm

Chris Ofili

133

Jonathan Parsons

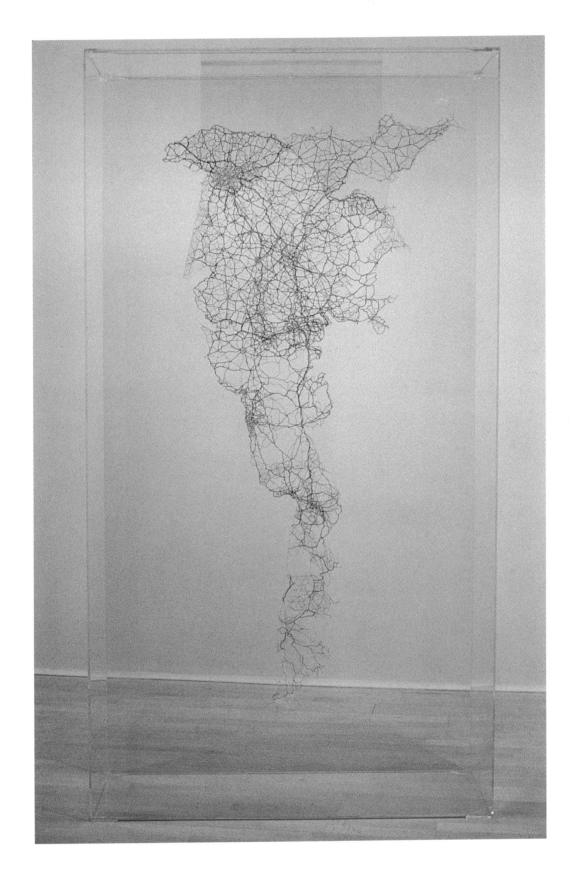

Carcass | 1995 | dissected map in acrylic case, 200 x 110 x 40 cm

Richard Patterson

Blue Minotaur | 1996 | oil on canvas, 208 x 312.4 cm

Richard Patterson

Culture Station #2 – Dirty Picture | 1996 | oil on canvas, 213.3 x 427.7 cm

Richard Patterson

Motorcrosser II | 1995 | oil and acrylic on canvas, 208 x 315 cm

Richard Patterson

Culture Station #3 – With Fur Hat | 1997 | oil on canvas, 213.3 x 427.7 cm

Richard Patterson

141

Simon Patterson

The Great Bear | 1992 | four-colour lithographic print in anodised aluminium frame, 109 x 134.8 x 5 cm

Hadrian Pigott

Instrument of Hygiene (case 1) | 1995 | fibreglass, leatheret covering, velvet lining, with wash basin and fittings, 90 x 50 x 43 cm

Marc Quinn

Self | 1991 | blood, stainless steel, perspex, refrigeration equipment, 208 x 63 x 63 cm

The Morphology of Specifics | 1996 | glass and silver, dimensions variable

Marc Quinn

148

No Visible Means of Escape | 1996 | RTV 74-30, rope , 180.3 x 59.7 x 30.5 cm

Marc Quinn

Fiona Rae

Untitled (Sky Shout) | 1997 | oil and acrylic on canvas, 274.3 x 243.8 cm

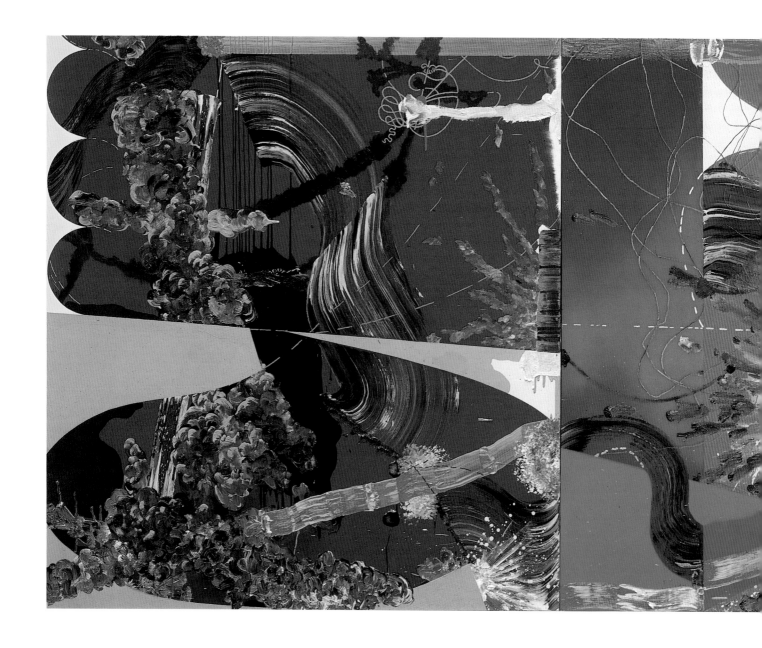

Fiona Rae

Untitled (blue and purple triptych) | 1994 | oil on canvas, 183 x 502.9 cm

Fiona Rae

153

Untitled (purple and brown) | 1991 | oil and charcoal on canvas, 198 x 213.4 cm

Fiona Rae

154

Untitled (one on brown) | 1989 | oil on canvas, 213.4 x 198 cm

Fiona Rae

·155

James Rielly

Random Acts of Kindness | 1996
oil on canvas, overall size 290 x 410 cm

Jenny Saville

Propped | 1992 | oil on canvas, 213.5 x 183 cm

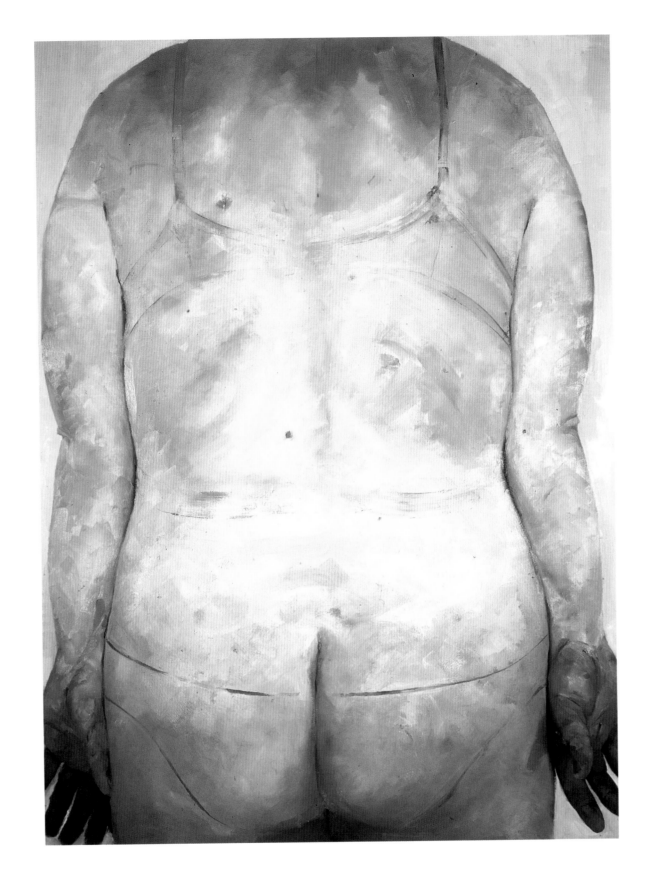

Trace | 1993–4 | oil on canvas, 213.5 x 182.8 cm

Jenny Saville

160

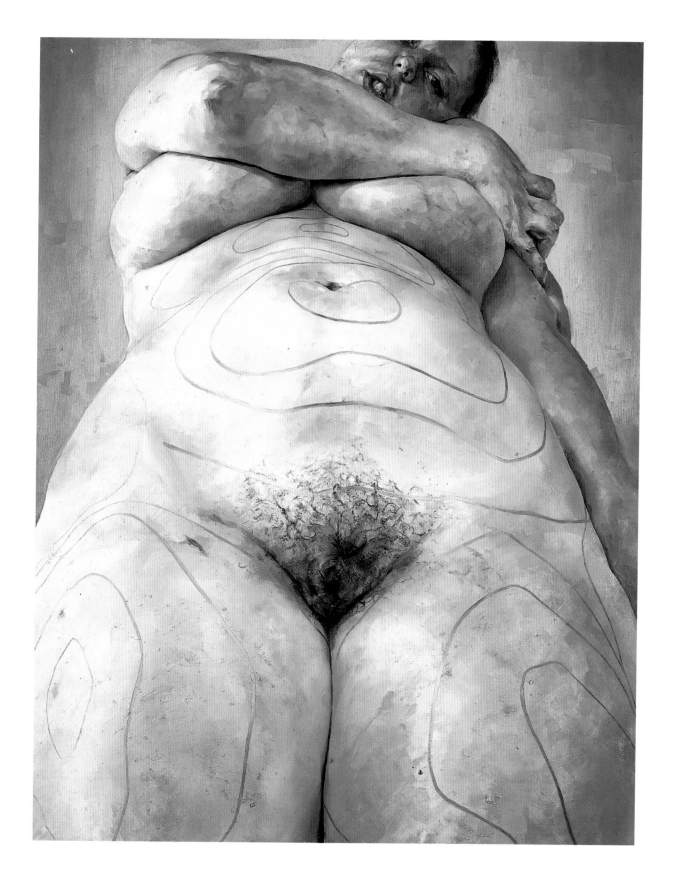

Plan | 1993 | oil on canvas, 274 x 213.5 cm

Jenny Saville

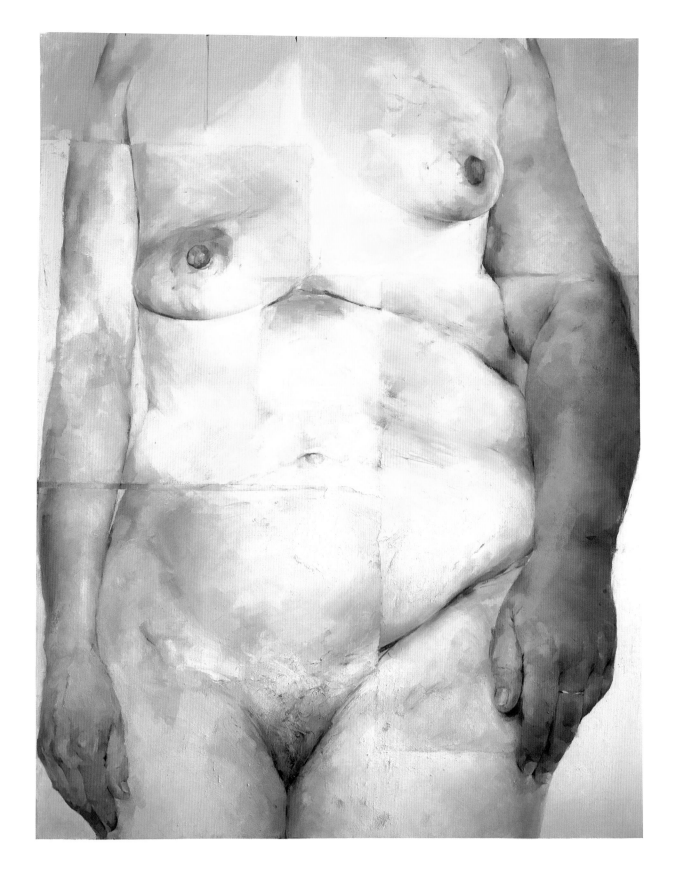

Hybrid | 1997 | oil on canvas, 274.3 x 213.4 cm

Jenny Saville

162

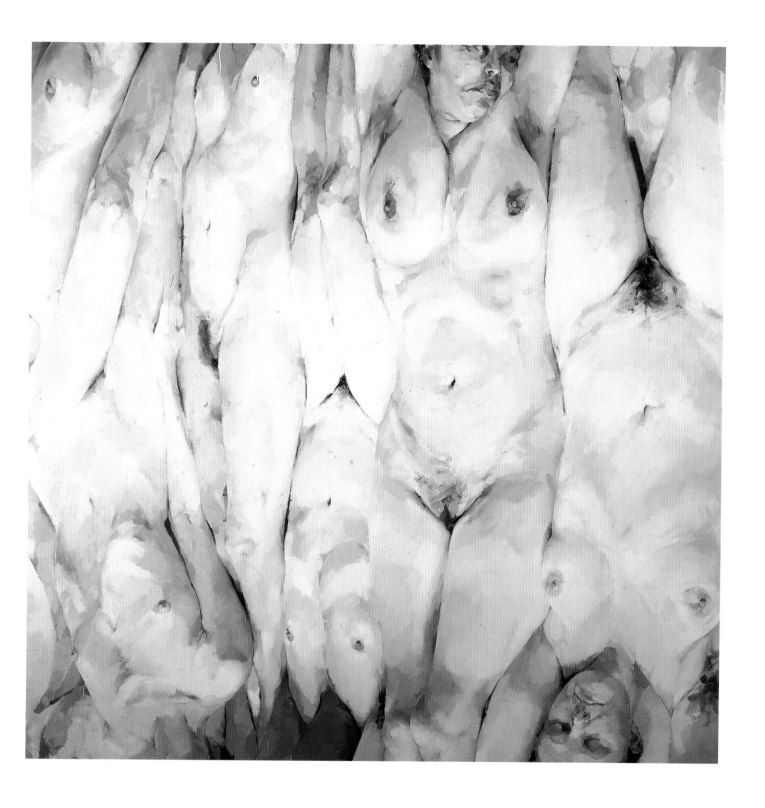

Shift | 1996–7 | oil on canvas, 330 x 330 cm

Jenny Saville

163

Yinka Shonibare

How Does a Girl Like You, Get to Be a Girl Like You? | 1995 | wax print cotton textiles, 168 x 40 cm approx

Jane Simpson

Sacred | 1993 | MDF, gesso, watercolour, tinplate, refrigeration unit, 112.5 x 127.5 x 55 cm

Sam Taylor-Wood

Killing Time | 1994 | video projection and sound, duration 60 minutes

Sam Taylor-Wood

Above • **Five Revolutionary Seconds I** | 1995 | colour photograph, 21 x 200 cm
Centre • **Five Revolutionary Seconds III** | 1996 | colour photograph, 20.5 x 200 cm
Below • **Five Revolutionary Seconds VII** | 1997 | colour photograph, 29.5 x 200 cm

Sam Taylor-Wood

Sam Taylor-Wood

Wrecked | 1996 | C-type colour print, 152.4 x 396.2 cm

Sam Taylor-Wood

173

Gavin Turk

Pop | 1993 | glass, brass, MDF, fibreglass, wax, clothing, gun, 279 x 115 x 115 cm

Mark Wallinger

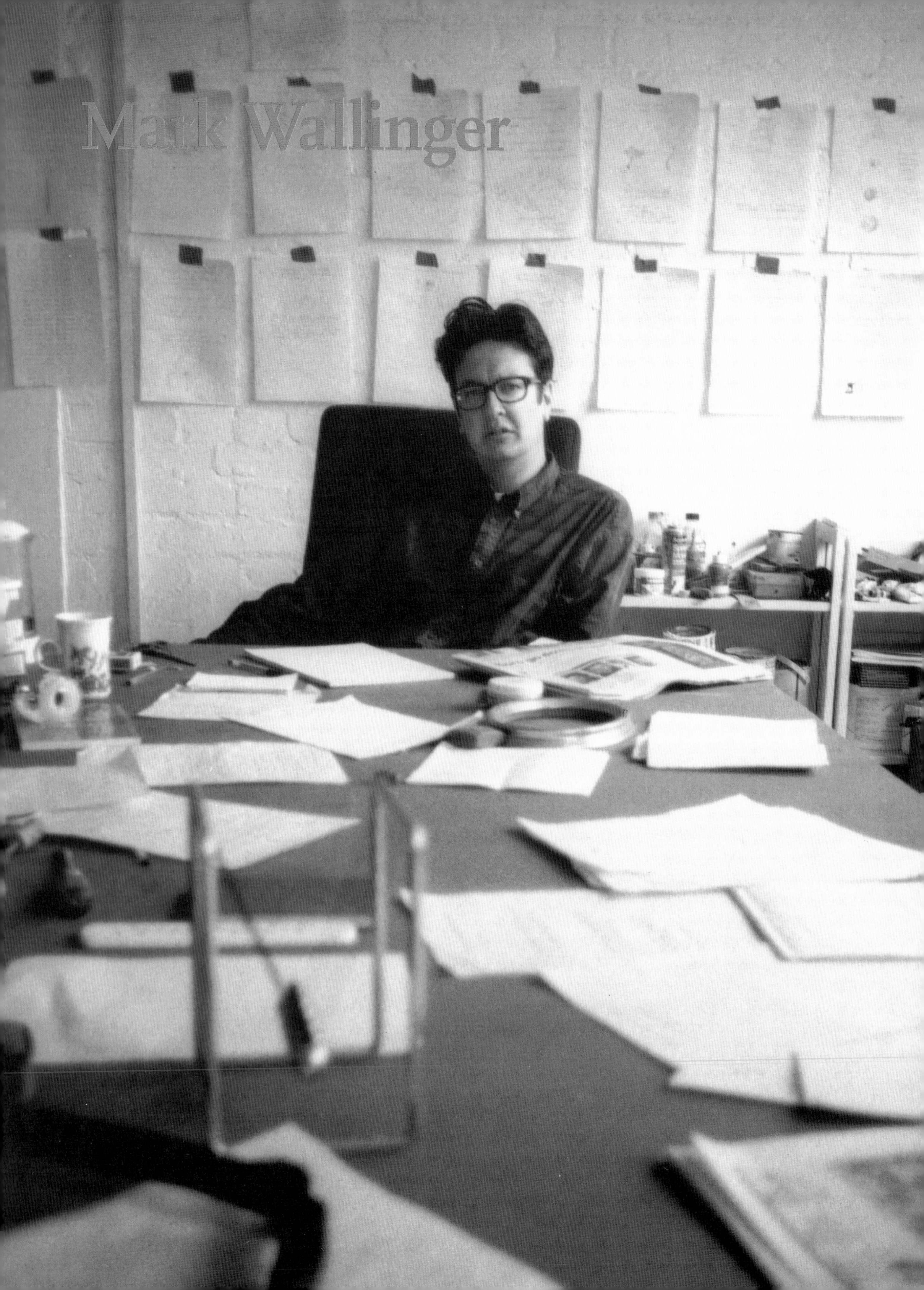

Angel | 1997 | video/laserdisc, duration 7 minutes 30 seconds

Mark Wallinger

178

Race Class Sex | 1992 | oil on canvas, each 230 x 300 cm

Mark Wallinger

Gillian Wearing

10 - 16 | 1997 | video projection, duration 15 minutes

Rachel Whiteread

Untitled (Bath) | 1990 | plaster, glass, 103 x 209.5 x 105.5cm
Overleaf · **Ghost** | 1990 | plaster on steel frame, 269 x 355.5 x 317.5 cm

Untitled (Square Sink) | 1990 | plaster, 107 x 101 x 86.5 cm

Rachel Whiteread

Untitled (Orange Bath) | 1996 | rubber, polystyrene, 80 x 207 x 110 cm
Overleaf · **Untitled (One-Hundred Spaces)** | 1995 | resin, 100 units, dimensions variable

Rachel Whiteread

187

Cerith Wyn Evans

Inverse Reverse Perverse | 1996 | surface mirrored acrylic, diameter 73 cm

Darren Almond | Born Wigan, 1971

For the 'Something Else' show at Exmouth Market, London, in 1996, Darren Almond video projected a live broadcast via satellite from his West London studio into the exhibition space. In his studio above his desk on the wall, an amplified industrial flip-clock menacingly kept time. With the clock as the only witness to the absence of the artist, and of artistic activity of any kind, the work challenged the notion of the artist's studio as the site *par excellence* of creative production.

In 1995, in a work called *KN120*, Almond installed a large white ceiling fan underneath London's Westway with an extension cord hooked up to the mains in his studio. Almond also used a fan in his recent one-person show at White Cube, London: an installation for which he hung an over-sized ceiling fan in the centre of the space and carpeted the gallery's floor. The fan was equipped with extended blades that almost reached the four walls of the gallery, creating a surreal yet sinister environment.

Almond was awarded the prestigious ICA/Toshiba Art & Innovation Prize in 1996. In 1997 he created an installation entitled *HMP Pentonville* at the ICA, London, in which he broadcast live from an empty prison cell into the gallery. The work invites the viewer to witness the monotony of time that is the isolation of prison life. It also questions broadcasting as a mode of narrative: the only action we see is the changing of natural light in the cell, and the sounds of the prison itself.

Darren Almond graduated from the Winchester School of Art in 1994. He participated in Gregor Muir's show, 'A Small Shifting Sphere of Serious Culture', at the ICA in 1996.

Bussel

Maria Alvarez, 'Darren Almond: An artist whose work is industrial-strength', *Telegraph Magazine*, February 1997.

Martin Herbert, 'Doing Time', *Dazed and Confused*, 29, 1997, pp. 80–3.

Sarah Kent, 'Darren Almond', *Time Out*, 26 February–5 March 1997, p. 51.

Richard Billingham | Born Birmingham, 1970

Richard Billingham graduated from the University of Sunderland in 1994, the same year that he took part in his first group exhibition at the Barbican Art Gallery, London. For seven years Billingham had taken photographs of his parents, brother and pets in their Sunderland estate flat, initially as studies for paintings. Then, with the help of a photography editor friend, he began showing these 'studies', which have now been exhibited to great acclaim at galleries in New York, Milan and Paris, as well as at Anthony Reynolds in London. They have also been made into a book entitled *Ray's A Laugh*.

Billingham's photographs have been hailed as a mass of contradictions. They are as naïve, humane and beautiful as they are artificial, raw and disconcerting. They lie somewhere between documentary and fiction. As an obvious insider, Billingham is as much spectator as actor in this tragicomedy of domestic life.

Against the grain of traditional British propriety, the photographs are a warts-and-all depiction of a disconsolate working class family. Billingham's parents, Ray and Liz, are the primary focus of the pictures. Seen through the camera's lens, they are at once heroic and lamentable. In one image we see Liz handing Ray a plate of food; his arms are extended and a thankful smile lights up his face. In another, Ray, a chronic alcoholic, is witnessed passed out on the bathroom floor, his vomit covering the toilet seat. Still another shot shows Liz nursing a puppy with a syringe, supported by her large tattooed arm. Whether violent, miserable, or endearing, Billingham's photographs evince the artist's understanding of his subjects' spiritedness in their ineluctable situation.

Bussel

Gordon Burn, 'Common People', *Guardian*, 30 March, 1996, pp. 17–19.

Mark Sanders, 'Interview with Richard Billingham', *Dazed and Confused*, 22, July 1996, pp. 60–4.

Gilda Williams, 'Richard Billingham', *Art Monthly*, 199, September 1996, pp. 31–2.

Glenn Brown | Born Hexham, 1966

In 1989, a year after graduating from the Bath Academy of Art, Glenn Brown was selected for the 'BT New Contemporaries', a high-profile touring exhibition of young artists. A year later – now beginning his MA at Goldsmiths College – he was again selected for this exhibition.

Brown's manner of working is typical of the generation of artists coming out of colleges, particularly Goldsmiths, at that time: visually direct, professionally constructed, and theoretically adept. Many younger artists were also then finding a personal style (what once would have been called their 'mature style') and rigorously ploughing their own furrow. His distinctive paintings, which appropriate well-known works and reconstruct them in a painstakingly hyper-real manner, was quickly gaining recognition. However, during the 1994 exhibition 'Here and Now' at the Serpentine Gallery, they acquired a degree of notoriety. A series of paintings that took works by Salvador Dali as their starting point had to be pulled from the exhibition under threat of legal action by the Dali Foundation. But the incident generated a lot of publicity for Brown and, what is more, made explicit many of the questions that he intended his works to raise.

Having received a great deal of attention in that exhibition, Brown went on to his first solo show at Karsten Schubert Gallery in 1995, and then to many survey shows, such as 'From Here' (1995), 'About Vision' (1996), and the young British artists' exhibition 'Brilliant!' in Minneapolis, 1995.

Barrett

LONDON 1995. *From Here*, exhibition catalogue by Andrew Wilson, Waddington and Karsten Schubert galleries, London, 1995.
MINNEAPOLIS 1995. *Brilliant! New Art From London*, exhibition catalogue by Douglas Fogle, Walker Art Center, Minneapolis, 1995.
Stuart Morgan, 'Confessions of a Body Snatcher', *Frieze*, 12, 1993.

Simon Callery | Born London, 1960

After completing his studies at the Cardiff College of Art in 1983, Simon Callery did not exhibit his work publicly until 1989. That was in the high-profile 'Whitechapel Open' at the Whitechapel Gallery, London, an exhibition in which he was invited to show again in 1990 and 1992. He presented his first solo show, at the Free Trade Wharf, in 1991, and was also included that year in 'Collector's Eye' at the Fruitmarket Gallery, Edinburgh. By then, Callery's painting style was becoming distinctive: washes of pale colour layered with softly drafted lines, evoking the skies seen from the window of a high building.

After spending part of 1992 as Artist in Residence at Camden Arts Centre, Callery went on to present two solo shows at the Anderson O'Day Gallery, in 1993 and 1994. Works of his were included in the 1993 group shows 'Strictly Painting' at the Cubitt Gallery, and 'John Moores 18' at the Walker Art Gallery, Liverpool, in which he was a prizewinner, while 1994 saw him included in group shows in Turin, Italy, as well as presenting a solo show there at the Galleria Christian Stein. In 1996 Callery had a solo exhibition at Anthony Wilkinson Fine Art, and his work was shown in 'About Vision' at the Museum of Modern Art, Oxford, and the Courtauld Institute's East Wing Collection.

In 1997 Callery is participating in 'Pure Fantasy' at Oriel Mostyn, Llandudno, Wales, 'Experiment GB' at the Kunstverein Trier & Kubus in Hannover, Germany, and also the touring exhibition 'A Cloudburst of Material Possessions'. Callery's major solo project of 1997 is 'The Segsbury Project' at The Great Barn, Farringdon, and the University and Pitt Rivers Museums, Oxford.

Barrett

Simon Morley, 'Simon Callery', *Art Monthly*, April 1993.
Simon Morley, 'The Sublime and the Beautiful', *Art Monthly*, June 1996.
LONDON 1996. *Una Veste di Colore*, exhibition catalogue by Christopher Bucklow, Anthony Wilkinson Fine Art, London, 1996.

Jake & Dinos Chapman
Jake Chapman | Born Cheltenham, 1966
Dinos Chapman | Born London, 1962

Jake & Dinos Chapman have been a collaborative team since the early 1990s. Their first solo installation, 'We Are Artists', was an aesthetic manifesto of sorts, made with Letraset on a wall covered in excrement-like brown paint. The following year, they created a diorama sculpture out of remodelled plastic figurines enacting scenes from Goya's *Disasters of War* series of etchings of the early 19th century. A single scene from the work was then meticulously transformed into a life-size tableau with refashioned generic fibreglass mannequins.

In *Great Deeds Against the Dead* (1994, p. 65) three castrated soldiers in various states of bodily mutilation are tied to a tree. The Chapmans' reappropriation of Goya's solemn etching becomes an ironic evocation of beauty and perversity, humour and horror.

Over the past few years the Chapmans have further exploited the shop-window dummy. *Zygotic acceleration, biogenetic, de-sublimated libidinal model (enlarged x 1000)* (1995, p. 67) is a ring of kitsch child mannequins with joined torsos, sporting wigs and Fila trainers.

These blue-eyed, nubile figures are also connected by gaping vaginas, or have a penis and anus in lieu of a nose and mouth. The same mutant creatures are present in the installation *Tragic Anatomies* (1996, pp. 68–9). They are genderless, self-reproducing manifestations of excess libidinal energy gone awry.

Jake & Dinos Chapman both graduated from the Royal College of Art. They have recently had solo exhibitions at the ICA, London, Grazer Kunstverein, Graz, Austria, and Gagosian Gallery, New York.

Bussel

LONDON 1996. *Chapmanworld*, exhibition catalogue with essays by David Falconer, Douglas Fogle and Nick Land, ICA, London, 1996.
Stuart Morgan, 'Rude Awakening', *Frieze*, 19, November/December 1994, pp. 30–3.
Mark Sanders, 'The Art World Deserves Them', *Dazed & Confused*, 14, October 1995, pp. 54–7.

Adam Chodzko | Born London, 1965

Adam Chodzko is interested in the margins of society. His work focuses on subcultures that possess their own vernacular, identity and meaning. Through the ad pages of *Loot* magazine, Chodzko enters into a symbolic system of correspondence which fleshes out collective fantasies through the language of commodity exchange: uniting diverse people within a shared context.

Transmitters is an ongoing project, started in 1990, in which Chodzko places fake advertisements in *Loot*. He uses real artists' names to sell 'works' that would have little use value outside the rarefied world of the art market. *Certainly* (1992) is a collection of telephone messages from readers of the personal columns that Chodzko has 'matched up', illustrating the 'equal balance of the desiring and the desired'.

For *God Look-Alike Contest* (1992–3, p. 71) Chodzko placed a notice in magazines all over the world looking for people who believe they resemble God. The resulting piece is a collection of twelve framed images (plus the announcement) of people from all over the world who indeed feel they look like or embody the Almighty: a naked woman, a young couple from Minsk, and a woman from Ghana standing in front of a car. Here Chodzko underlines the identical fantasy of a globally diverse group of people.

Recently Chodzko has used a 'contact' magazine for *Involva* (1995) to solicit readers' responses to a drawing of a forest and the line 'Please will you join me'. The obliging letters he received were then photographed in an actual forest, conflating the respondents' fantasies with the forest as a site of fantasy.

Adam Chodzko graduated from Goldsmiths College in 1994. He has recently had solo exhibitions at Lotta Hammer, London, and Fontanella Borghes, Rome. He has also participated in shows at De Appel, Amsterdam, and at the Hayward Gallery, London.

Bussel

David Burrows, 'Adam Chodzko', *Art Monthly*, 198, July–August 1996, pp. 28–9.
James Roberts, 'Adult Fun', *Frieze*, 31, November/December 1996, pp. 62–7.
Kate Spicer, 'Nearly God', *The Face*, 93, June 1996, pp. 94–8.

Mat Collishaw | Born Nottingham, 1966

While studying for his BA at Goldsmiths College (1986–9), Mat Collishaw was invited to contribute to the 1988 'Freeze' exhibition at Surrey Docks, now considered to be the ground-zero exhibition for British art of the 1990s. From such a public beginning he went on to contribute to group exhibitions in Italy (the 'Aperto' section of the Venice Bienniale, 1993), Austria, Switzerland, France ('L'Hiver de l'amour', 1994, and 'Live/Life', 1996, both at the Musée d'Art Moderne), the USA ('Brilliant!', Walker Art Center, Minneapolis, 1995), Holland, Greece, Turkey, Portugal, Canada, Germany, and of course London, where selected shows have included 'Modern Medicine', Building One (1990), 'Institute of Cultural Anxiety', ICA (1994), 'Minky Manky', South London Gallery, 'Here & Now', Serpentine Gallery and 'The British Art Show 4' (all 1995), and 'The Inner Eye' at Manchester City Art Gallery (1996).

Collishaw's work has changed considerably since he first came to prominence, when he was known primarily for his work *Bullet Hole*, which presented advertising light-boxes displaying a close-up image of a head wound. More recently he has been associated with images of nature that have been digitally manipulated to construct alternative fantasy worlds. From his first solo show in London, at Karsten Schubert in 1990, Collishaw has gone on to present solo shows in the USA, France, Switzerland and Italy, as well as back in London, such as at the Camden Arts Centre in 1995.

Barrett

Andrew Renton and Liam Gillick (eds), *Technique Anglaise: Current Trends in British Art*, London and New York, 1991.
Julian Stallabrass, 'Mat Collishaw', *Art Monthly*, February 1991.
Stuart Morgan, 'Forbidden Images', *Frieze*, 26, 1996.

Keith Coventry | Born Burnley, 1958

In 1981, the year he completed his BA degree at Brighton Polytechnic, Keith Coventry was selected to exhibit in the first of his many group shows, 'Northern Young Contemporaries' at the Whitworth Gallery in Manchester. This was the same year that he began his MA at Chelsea School of Art, London, a course he completed in 1982, fully ten years before his first solo show, 'Ivory Towers' at Karsten Schubert, London. However, during that decade he exhibited at City Racing, an artist-run space that included Coventry among its organisers. In 1992 these City Racing artists exhibited together in a group show at the Transmission Gallery, Glasgow, and Coventry was also involved that year in group shows in both New York and San Francisco.

In 1993 Coventry's solo shows 'Suprematist Painting I–X' and 'Recent Works' were seen at Karsten Schubert; the latter also toured to the USA. His *Suprematist Paintings* are easily recognised, for they mimic works by Malevich and Rodchenko, but use plan views of council estates to generate their block patterns. The group show 'World Cup Football Karaoke', curated by Georg Herold at the Portikus in Frankfurt in 1994, included Coventry among its partici-pants. He also exhibited his *White Abstracts* in 1994 at Karsten Schubert, and then in 1995 at the Curt Marcus Gallery in New York. The survey painting show 'From Here', held at Waddington and Karsten Schubert in 1995, contained Coventry's *White Abstract (Winston Churchill, After Graham Sutherland)*, in which a portrait of Churchill was painted in various shades of white. Coventry's most recent solo show was at the Spacex Gallery, Exeter, in 1997.
Barrett

LONDON 1994. *Keith Coventry—White Abstracts*, exhibition catalogue by Andrew Wilson, Karsten Schubert, London, 1994.
William Furlong, 'Interview: Keith Coventry, Nov 1994', *Audio Arts Magazine*, June 1995.
Carl Freedman, 'Keith Coventry', *Frieze*, 35, 1997.

Peter Davies | Born Edinburgh, 1970

Peter Davies makes obsessional paintings about the medium of paint-ing itself: technique, style and artistic inheritance are his subject-matter. The work is at once fastidious and awkward, painted in a *faux-naïf* style, and a knowing conceit on self-referentiality.

Text Painting (1996, p. 77) was first shown as part of the 'Die Yuppie Scum' show, curated by Martin Maloney at Karsten Schubert, London. The painting is a large-format scrawl listing Davies's favourite artists and their importance to him; it immediately brings to mind the American artist Sean Landers and his neurotic art-nerd musings. Davies uses random multicoloured letters, creating a sea of thought that reads as an ironic paean to such contemporary artists as Anthony Caro ('now he really is one mean badass M.F. S.O.B.'...), Damien Hirst, Sarah Lucas and Gilbert and George, as well as Warhol, Beuys and Matisse.

For 'Gothic' at Lost in Space, London, Davies created a large text painting, again with letters written in alternating colours, which listed all the artists he thought of as Gothic, and why. *Small Square Painting* (1996) is an enormous multicoloured work, obsessively executed yet haphazard in design, that creates the perception of a vibrating mosaic of tiny square blocks of colour.

Peter Davies graduated from Goldsmiths College in 1996. In 1997 he participated in the 'Artists and their Spread' exhibition at 53 Exmouth Market, London, and was also commissioned by Habitat Kings Road, London, to make a work entitled *Small Circle Painting*.
Bussel

Matthew Collings, *Blimey! From Bohemia to Britpop: The London Artworld from Francis Bacon to Damien Hirst*, London, 1997, pp. 13, 142.
Martin Coomer, 'Gothic', *Time Out*, 6–13 December 1995, p. 52.
Ben Judd, 'Die Yuppie Scum', *Untitled*, 11, Summer 1996.

Tracey Emin | Born London, 1963

Tracey Emin's art appears as a tautology: her art is her life, her history, and vice versa. It has meaning only insofar as Emin herself does. She recreates her past, memorialises it, and weaves it into a narrative performance. Casting herself as the star of her own seriocomic life, she literally re-inscribes it as objects: banners, quilts, chairs, bags, and a tent. She also makes videos, etchings and paintings, and writes books and poetry. Emin's autobiographical confessional is always open to the public as the divide between art and life is wilfully collapsed.

In 1993 Emin ran 'The Shop' – a kind of art boutique in East London – with artist Sarah Lucas. There they created objects such as a 'Rothko Comfort Blanket' and Damien-Hirst's-face ashtrays. In 1994 Emin had her first solo show at White Cube, London, entitled 'My Major Retrospective', where she exhibited her diaries, letters and memorabilia, as well as miniature photographs of her old paintings from college. This exhibition inaugurated Emin's art of confession as catharsis, with her charismatic narratives of pain, love, abuse and survival, subsequently evidenced in her birth-to-adolescence book *Explorations of the Soul*.

Everyone I Have Ever Slept With (1963–1995) (1995, p. 79) is a blue tent appliquéd with the names of Emin's bedmates – from family members and sexual partners to the foetus she aborted. The work is a kind of archaeology of variously intimate relations within the confines of a 'confessional' shelter. Also in 1995, Emin founded her eponymous Museum, located in Waterloo Road, London, as a site for her own exhibitions and performances.

Tracey Emin graduated from Maidstone College of Art in 1986. In 1997 she had a solo exhibition, entitled 'I Need Art Like I Need God', at the South London Gallery.

Bussel

Michael Corris, 'Tracey Emin', *Artforum*, February 1995, pp. 84–5.
David Lillington, 'Private View', *Time Out*, 1–7 December 1993.
Stuart Morgan, 'The Story of I', *Frieze*, 34, May 1997, pp. 56–61.

Paul Finnegan | Born London, 1968

Paul Finnegan creates sculptures and photographs that make manifest hallucinatory states of reality. The locus of his work is the figure, and by extension, the human form morphed beyond recognition into a kind of supernatural trace of itself.

Finnegan uses photography to explore the potential of his chimeric manifestations which are unrealisable as sculptures. In the series entitled *Spuriosis* (1995), phantasmic blobs seen from the inside of a car hang in the air of a once-benign country road, now made strikingly uncanny by their otherworldly presence. In a series of 'self-portraits', *Adaption* (1997), Finnegan's face becomes an hallucinogenic distortion of itself, with metallic and glass protuberances 'grafted' on to a disfigured countenance. The photographs look computer-generated, but are created by slide projection onto a distorted screen: a low-tech conceit that plays on the notion of process and illusion.

Finnegan's reinforced painted plastic sculptures are, like his photographs, supernatural transmogrifications of the human figure, rendered in dervish-like form. *Untitled* (1995, p. 81), is a grey, meringue-like, ectoplasmic creature sporting men's shoes. This menacing post-human is caught in suspended animation, a paranormal entity perturbing all our notions of the Real.

Paul Finnegan graduated from St Martin's School of Art in 1992. In 1993, he participated in 'Hiatus' at Metro Works, as well as 'Ideal Standard Summertime' at the Lisson Gallery, London. In summer 1997 he exhibited in the 'Avatars' show at Entwistle Gallery, London.

Bussel

Mark Sladen, 'The Body In Question', *Art Monthly*, 191, November 1995, pp. 3–5.

Mark Francis | Born Newtownards, Northern Ireland, 1962

Since graduating from the Chelsea School of Art, London, in 1986, Mark Francis has made paintings based on microbiological photographs of charged cellular structures. These large, technically rigorous, black, white and grey canvases (sometimes carrying traces of muted colour) are deliberately both abstract and figurative. The figures on their near-photographic, gestureless surfaces refer to the microscopic structures of blood, sperm, chromosomes and bacteria.

With titles such as *Scatter*, *Restriction* and *Displacement*, Francis's works evoke sublime states of alienation and sadness. His radically enlarged, almost sinister black squiggles and blobs exist in constant flux: they either cluster together in a collectivity or spread out over the blurred surface of the canvas as if trying to escape. These paintings are full of contradiction: they are at once frozen and kinetic, random and ordered, abstract and figurative.

As maps of human microscopic physiology, Francis's paintings emphasise the distance, created by technological apparatus, that separates us from our own bodies. They question our relationship to the physical world through an examination of our own foreign cellular structures. There is a sense of stasis in his pictures. They are staged in the act of of evolving into something other, a single moment in an unending, slow-motion osmosis.

Mark Francis has recently had solo exhibitions at Mary Boone Gallery, New York, and Anne de Villepoix in Paris. He has also shown at Interim Art and the Tate Gallery, London.

Bussel

Mark Durden, 'Mark Francis', *Frieze*, 22, May 1995, pp. 62–3.
David Lillington, 'Mark Francis', *Time Out*, 4–11 May 1994, p. 40.
Simon Morely, 'Mark Francis', *Art Monthly*, 187, June 1995, pp. 34–5.

Alex Hartley | Born 1963, West Byfleet

Alex Hartley's first exhibition was in Holland: 'International Departures' at Kavalere Kazerne, Amsterdam, in 1990. This was also the year that he graduated from the Royal College of Art, prior to which he had spent four years at the Camberwell School of Art. The 1991 'Whitechapel Open' gave Hartley his first chance to exhibit in London, followed later in the same year by the group shows 'Show Hide Show' and 'Crossover', both at the Anderson O'Day Gallery.

Hartley's constructions often involve photographs placed in boxes with ground-glass fronts, making them as difficult to look at as they are to look away from. On the strength of these works he was soon given solo shows, first at the Anderson O'Day Gallery (1992) and then at the Victoria Miro Gallery, and at James van Damme in Antwerp, Belgium (both 1993). 'Conceptual Living' at Rhizome in Amsterdam in 1995 was shown in the same year as another pair of solo shows, at Galerie Gilles Peyroulet, Paris, and again at Victoria Miro. By now Hartley's working methods were familiar, and his powerful steel-cased images of tower blocks were perfect for the Delfina Gallery's 'Inner London' show of 1996.

Hartley was represented in a spate of group shows in 1996, including 'Abstract/Real' at the Museum Moderner Kunst Stiftung Ludwig, Vienna; 'Wordt Vervoled' at Lumen Travo, Amsterdam; 'Espaces Constroits/Espace Critiques' in FRAC Basse, France; 'Fall Out' at Darmstadt, Germany; 'City Limits' at Staffordshire University and 'Spacious', with Willy de Sauter, at Battersea Arts Centre, London.

Barrett

Michael Bracewell, 'Someone to Watch Over Me', *Frieze*, 1, London, 1991.
LONDON 1992. *Keith Coventry*, exhibition catalogue by David Batchelor, Anderson O'Day Gallery, London, 1992.
Andrew Renton, 'Keith Coventry', *Flash Art*, Summer 1992.

Marcus Harvey | Born Leeds, 1963

Marcus Harvey makes disquieting, tension-filled paintings that simultaneously contain and exceed their salacious imagery. Through the superimposition of pornographic female nudes on to a wildly expressionistic ground, form and content resist and comply with each other uneasily.

Both pornography and Abstract Expressionism have been criticised as constructions of the imperious male gaze that frames and objectifies women. Harvey's large-scale paintings literally collapse and reframe these overdetermined genres, rendering them both equivocal. The dialectic of high and low art is made ambiguous, as vibrant splashy brushstrokes are combined with hard-edged outlines of erotic female crotch shots: de Kooning and DIY suburban erotica meet and cancel each other out.

In 1995 Harvey exhibited *Myra* (1995, p. 87), a portrait of child-murderer Myra Hindley. The work looks like a giant blow-up of a police photograph in steely black, white and grey. On closer inspection this already sinister image becomes all the more profane as one recognises that the dotted paint marks are actually children's handprints. *Proud of His Wife* (1994, p. 88) is a 'reader's wife' portrait of a headless woman with legs akimbo, painted with expressionistic fervour onto a floral background in lurid pink and magenta.

Marcus Harvey graduated from Goldsmiths College in 1986. He has had solo exhibitions at Vedovi Fine Art, Brussels, and White Cube, London. Harvey participated in 'About Vision: New British Painting' in the 1990s at the Museum of Modern Art, Oxford, as well as 'Young British Artists III' at the Saatchi Gallery, London, in 1995.

Bussel

Richard Dorment, 'Could this be the real thing?', *Daily Telegraph*, 5 April, 1995, p. 18.
Sarah Kent, *Shark Infested Waters: The Saatchi Collection of British Art in the 90s*, London, 1994.
Adrian Searle, 'Marcus Harvey', *Time Out*, 26 January–2 February, 1994, p. 42.

Mona Hatoum | Born Beirut, Lebanon, 1952

Mona Hatoum is a Palestinian exile who has been living in London since 1975. After studying at the Slade School of Art she began making video and performance art. Her work deals with the contradictions of power and identity. Since the late 1980s, Hatoum has made large-scale environmental installations involving sculpture, video and sound.

With *Light at the End* (1989), Hatoum created a dark, foreboding tunnel space illuminated by red tubular heat lamps – a no-exit situation. In 1992 she produced *Light Sentence* at the Museum of Modern Art in New York. A pun on the legal term, the work – an environment made of metal cages with a swinging light hung at its centre – evoked a feeling of imprisonment, with its searchlight moving endlessly like a pendulum.

In 1994 Hatoum had a one-person exhibition at the Pompidou Centre in Paris. There she showed *Socle du Monde* (Pedestal of the Earth), a giant magnetised cube covered in iron filings, which plays on the uncertainty of the surface of destabilised lives. In the same year, Hatoum made *Corps Etranger* for the Tate Gallery, an overhead video projection contained within a large cylindrical edifice. This showed the artist's body inside and out, filmed with an endoscope and projected onto the floor, accompanied by the sound of her heartbeat, pulse and breath. For *Deep Throat* (1996, p. 91), Hatoum presented a dining-table with tablecloth, setting and chair. Back-projected through the plate is an endoscopic video of the artist's larynx expanding and contracting, making the physical act of eating uncomfortably real.

Mona Hatoum has exhibited throughout the world. She has recently had solo shows at the Museum of Contemporary Art in Chicago, and at De Appel in Amsterdam.

Bussel

Laurel Berger, 'Mona Hatoum In Between, Outside & in the Margins', *Artnews*, September 1994, p. 149.

Dan Cameron, 'Mona Hatoum', *Artforum*, April 1993, p. 92.

Katy Deepwell, 'Inside Mona Hatoum', *Tate*, 6, Summer 1995, pp. 32–5.

Damien Hirst | Born Bristol, 1965

Damien Hirst curated the widely acclaimed 'Freeze' exhibition in 1988 while still a student at Goldsmiths College. This show launched the careers of many successful young British artists, including his own. Hirst graduated from Goldsmiths in 1989, and has since become the most famous living British artist after David Hockney.

In 1991, Hirst presented *In and Out of Love*, an installation for which he filled a gallery with hundreds of live tropical butterflies, some spawned from monochrome canvases on the wall. With *The Physical Impossibility of Death in the Mind of Someone Living* (1991, p. 93), his infamous tiger shark in a glass tank of formaldehyde shown at the Saatchi Gallery, Damien Hirst became a media icon and household name. He has since been imitated, parodied, reproached and exalted by the media and public alike.

Hirst's work is an examination of the processes of life and death: the ironies, falsehoods and desires that we mobilise to negotiate our own alienation and mortality. His production can be roughly grouped into three areas: paintings, cabinet sculptures and the glass tank pieces. The paintings divide into spot and spin paintings. The former are randomly organised, colour-spotted canvases with titles that refer to pharmaceutical chemicals. The spin paintings are 'painted' on a spinning table, so that each individual work is created through centrifugal force. For the cabinet series Hirst displayed collections of surgical tools or hundreds of pill bottles on highly ordered shelves. The tank pieces incorporate dead and sometimes dissected animals – cows, sheep or the shark – preserved in formaldehyde, suspended in death.

In 1997 Damien Hirst had a one-person exhibition at Bruno Bischofberger, Zurich, and has shown work at Gagosian Gallery, New York, and White Cube, London.

Bussel

Francesci Bonami, 'Damien Hirst', *Flash Art*, 189, Summer 1996, pp. 112–16.

Sarah Kent, *Shark Infested Waters: The Saatchi Collection of British Art in the 90s*, London, 1994.

NEW YORK 1996. Damien Hirst, *No Sense of Absolute Corruption*, exhibition catalogue, with interiew by Stuart Morgan, Gagosian Gallery, New York, 1996.

Gary Hume | Born Kent, 1962

Gary Hume graduated from Goldsmiths College in 1988, and is part of a generation of artists who have become internationally recognised since their participation in Damien Hirst's 'Freeze' exhibition in London's Docklands. Hume's work can be divided into two phases: the *Door* series, influenced by the Conceptual-based art practices of the '60s and '70s, and the subsequent Pop-inspired paintings. Until 1993 Hume worked on a suite of paintings resembling hospital swing doors: pairs of rectangles with circular and square windows (pp. 102–3). These paintings were executed in high gloss enamel on canvas or aluminium panels. They are schematic explorations of transitional space: connections between spaces, but not places in themselves. Their highly lacquered surfaces are reflective, putting the viewer both inside and outside the institutional doors.

With *This Is Not Possible* (1993), an abstracted figuration of the Madonna and Child, Hume gave up the rigorous formalism of his earlier work, freeing himself to make ambiguous yet sumptuously decorative paintings. Hume's images are culled from magazines and books, and are rendered in vibrant enamel paint on large aluminium panels. They incorporate everything from 'cut out' figures of pop icons Kate Moss and Patsy Kensit, to flowers and biomorphic blobs. In *Begging For It* (1994, p. 101), a pale blue figure is silhouetted against an avocado-green background, with jet-black arms and clasped hands reaching up, beseeching someone for something.

Gary Hume has exhibited widely in Britain and abroad, notably with White Cube in London and Matthew Marks in New York. In 1996 he was the British representative at the São Paulo Biennale, and was nominated for the Turner Prize. He has also had one-person exhibitions at Bonnefantenmuseum in Maastricht and the ICA in London.

Bussel

Adrian Dannatt, 'Gary Hume: The Luxury of Doing Nothing', *Flash Art*, 183, Summer 1995, pp. 97–9.

BERN 1995. *Gary Hume*, exhibition catalogue, Kunsthalle Bern/ICA London, 1995.

Gregor Muir, 'Lacquer Syringe', *Parkett*, 48, 1996, pp. 22–6.

Michael Landy | Born London, 1963

Michael Landy is interested in representing the relationship between art and the circulation of commodities. He uses found objects such as market carts and stalls, trolleys and rubbish bins to comment on the commodification of art and artists within a system of exchange, relating this to the selling of everyday goods.

In 1990, Landy created *Market,* a large installation in an East London warehouse. Throughout the space, street merchants' stalls and crates were set up. Fake grass carpets were hung over greengrocers' tiered steel frames. However, here there was no produce for sale: only the presentation displays themselves. For Landy, the 'apparatus of display' is the art.

Costermonger's Stall (1992–7, p. 109) is an old-fashioned blue and red mobile display unit. Buckets of colourful flowers are arranged on its tiered shelves, and light bulbs are festooned along its plastic yellow roof. The cart is an emblem of the past, much as its use-value has been short-circuited in the space of a gallery.

For *Closing Down Sale* (1992), Landy filled a gallery with shop trolleys of goods such as appliances and toys. The gallery walls were littered with day-glo signs reading 'Meltdown Madness Sale', 'Out of Business', or 'Everything Must Go'. An audiotape loop harangued visitors to 'Come on In' and 'Buy Now'. Landy had transformed the gallery into a high-street budget shop where artist and advertiser were conflated, and where the use-value of objects was rendered immaterial through their presentation as art. *Scrapheap Services* (1996), an installation at Chisenhale Gallery, London, examined the notions of human disposability and redundancy in a multi-national corporate world. In the gallery, uniformed mannequins cleaned up off the floor miniature human figures made of tin cans and fast food containers. In the corner of the space a large waste-disposal machine waited to shred the 'human' detritus to pieces.

Michael Landy graduated from Goldsmiths College in 1988. He has recently had solo exhibitions at the Henry Moore Foundation, Leeds, and Waddington Galleries, London. He participated in 'Brilliant! New Art from London' at the Walker Art Center, Minneapolis in 1995, as well as 'Ace' at the Hayward Gallery, London, in 1996.

Bussel

Joshua Decter, 'New York in Review', *Arts Magazine*, October 1991, p. 95.

Robin Dutt, 'Michael Landy', *What's On In London*, 20–7 May, 1992, p. 30.

Andrew Graham-Dixon, 'Thrown on the Scrapheap', *Independent*, 9 July, 1996, p. 12.

Abigail Lane | Born Penzance, 1967

Abigail Lane's work is concerned with the representation of the trace, and with the potentiality of clues or forensic evidence. The trace or imprint provides an identity, one that can be both artistic subject in itself and the clue to an event that might have taken place. Along with evidence there is always a story, a narrative of some sort. Lane's work offers up only the clues, leaving the viewer to imaginatively reconstruct this history for him- or herself.

In the early 1990s Lane created oversized, aluminium-encased, ink-pad diptychs. The pads, which evoke the work of Mark Rothko and Yves Klein, need constant re-inking, and are therefore continuously being 'remade' as artworks. With *Blue Print* (1992), the artist took a standard wooden chair and fitted it with a blue ink-pad cushion. The chair was positioned facing a wall on which hung a framed impression of a model's buttocks made by sitting on this chair, creating a circular logic and undermining the conventional subject/object relationship between viewer and artwork.

One of Lane's most ambitious shows to date, staged at the ICA, was 'Skin of the Teeth'. Along with an over-sized ink-pad piece, Lane dressed the gallery's wall in wallpaper printed with bloodprints copied from a police photograph of a vicious murder scene in New York City. In the middle of the space on the floor stood a concrete replica of a stuffed dog, its ears alert, waiting for the viewer to unpack the mystery of the crime. Also included in the show was a sculpture of human forearms and a head, mouth open as if emitting the last silent scream of the victim in this fictional crime scene.

Abigail Lane participated in Damien Hirst's 'Freeze' exhibition in 1988, and graduated from Goldsmiths College in 1989. In 1996, Lane had a one-person show at the Bonnefanten Museum in Maastricht. She recently participated in the 'Material Culture' exhibition at the Hayward Gallery, London.

Bussel

Alison Sarah Jacques, 'Abigail Lane: Body of Evidence', *Art + Text*, 54, 1996, pp. 56–61.

Sarah Kent, *Shark Infested Waters: The Saatchi Collection of British Art in the 90s*, London, 1994.

LONDON 1995. *Abigail Lane*, exhibition catalogue, ICA and Glen Scott Wright Contemporary Art, London, 1995.

Langlands & Bell

Ben Langlands | Born London, 1955
Nikki Bell | Born London, 1959

Ben Langlands and Nikki Bell graduated from Middlesex Polytechnic, London, in 1980, and have been collaborating ever since. Their work is an investigation of the relationship between people and architecture: the politics and aesthetics of space both as built environment and as idea. For the artists, notions of public and private construct our sense of self through the way our bodies negotiate (and are negotiated in) both the public and domestic sphere. Langlands & Bell are interested in the politics of that process.

Langlands & Bell's chairs and tables are metaphors for the body and society. Their minimalist white furniture acts as a link between ourselves and the architectonic spaces that both enable and constrain us. Models of institutional buildings such as prisons are encased within tables and chairs, conflating the boundaries between public and private, between bodies and organisms of power.

Architecture is a representation of social and economic values, and as such, building models are a kind of 'agenda', an ideological map. *Ivrea* (1991, p. 113) is a white-framed, three-dimensional cross-section of Ivrea, the utopian urban complex built by Olivetti outside Turin. The work seeks to 'amplify' the power relations of utopian architecture, which by collapsing industry with community has the effect of increasing control and regulation of both work and daily existence. Langlands & Bell have also made models of mosques, which, as sites of ritual, endlessly reproduce architecture's potential to create and transform subjectivity.

Langlands & Bell recently had solo exhibitions at the Serpentine Gallery, London, the Kunsthalle, Bielefeld, and at the Grey Art Gallery in New York.

Bussel

Sarah Kent, *Shark Infested Waters: The Saatchi Collection of British Art in the 90s*, London, 1994.
LONDON 1996. *Langlands & Bell*, exhibition catalogue by Germano Celant, with interview by Hans-Michael Herzog, Serpentine Gallery, London, 1996.

Sarah Lucas | Born London, 1962

Sarah Lucas graduated from Goldsmiths College in 1987, and participated in Damien Hirst's 'Freeze' show in 1988. Her sculptures are intended to provoke and amuse with their rough-hewn aesthetic and visual puns that examine gender in a tabloid-oriented society.

In the early 1990s, Lucas began using the *Sunday Sport* newspaper as source material, recontextualising its splashes on outrageous sex scandals and sensationalistic photographs of naked women. Her first solo show at City Racing, London, in 1992, was provocatively titled 'Penis Nailed to a Board'. The following year she participated in the 'Young British Artists II' show at the Saatchi Gallery, London, as well as setting up The Shop – an art multiples shop that she ran for six months with artist Tracey Emin.

Lucas often incorporates her own image into her work. She has made large-scale photographs and mobiles of herself as a self-conscious androgynous poseur. Along with her choice of everyday materials, Lucas also employs slang as part of her artistic vernacular. For *Two Fried Eggs and a Kebab* (1992, p. 116), she arranged the title's ingredients on top of a wooden table to represent a woman's breasts and genitalia, with a photograph of the work as its face. Whether it be profane or aggressive, Lucas's work is always undercut by a wry humour, as she consistently challenges our trash culture sensibilities.

In 1996 Lucas had a solo exhibition at the Museum Boymans-van Beuningen in Rotterdam, and was the subject of the BBC documentary *Two Melons and a Stinking Fish*. In 1997 she had a one-person show entitled 'The Law' with Sadie Coles HQ in London.

Bussel

Carl Freedman, 'A Nod's as Good as a Wink', *Frieze*, 17, June/July/August 1994, pp. 28–31.
ROTTERDAM 1996. *Sarah Lucas*, exhibition catalogue, Museum Boymans-van Beuningen, Rotterdam, 1996.
Jerry Saltz, 'She Gives as Good as She Gets', *Parkett*, 45, 1995, pp. 76–81.

Martin Maloney | Born London, 1961

Martin Maloney makes big bright 'bad' paintings of idle youth lounging, eating, listening to music, or watching television, whiling away the hours on a languid Sunday afternoon. The work is at once ironically naïve and wilfully expressive, with its awkward gestural strokes and unashamed sentimentality.

Maloney's work is an art-historical conceit as well as a labour of love. Earlier this year at Robert Prime, London, he created an exhibition called 'Genre Painting'. The title refers to 17th-century Spanish and Dutch paintings that depict simple scenes of domestic life. Maloney has radically updated this type of banal portraiture to include modern effects, such as laptop computers and a Sony cassette player. His cast of leisurely characters have all the time in the world to just sit around, chat on the telephone, or read the *Independent* newspaper. They are painted in flat broad gestures, and like their environments, conform to no rules of scale or perspective. Only the faces and eyes betray a sense of emotional gravity.

In *Bed Arrangements* (1997), a naked young man reclines in bed while his tawny-coloured cat – a hilarious-looking creature painted in thick brushstrokes – lies next to him. The impression is that they really have nothing better to do than lounge about all day and enjoy their trouble-free lives.

Maloney graduated from Goldsmiths College in 1993. In 1996 he had a one-person exhibition at Habitat Kings Road, London, and curated and participated in the 'Die Yuppie Scum' show at Karsten Schubert, London. Maloney also works as an art critic for *Flash Art* and *Artforum* magazines. He has curated a series of shows at Lost In Space, London, a gallery in his own home.

Bussel

Mark Currah, 'Martin Maloney', *Time Out*, 21–8 May 1997, p. 45.
Martin Herbert, 'Die Yuppie Scum', *Time Out*, 5–12 June 1996, p. 45.
John Windsor, 'Baddies With Brushes', *Independent on Sunday*, 20 October 1996, p. 86.

Jason Martin | Born Jersey, 1970

Graduating from the Foundation course at Chelsea School of Art in 1990, Jason Martin went on to the BA course at Goldsmiths College. In 1993, the year he completed his studies, Martin found himself in the young artists' survey show 'Wonderful Life' at the Lisson Gallery, and in a similar show a year later, 'The Curator's Egg', at the Anthony Reynolds Gallery. To say his painting technique is refined is an understatement: each of Martin's works is executed with a single stroke of the brush, producing a monochrome canvas. He constructs a special brush for each painting, always the same width as the canvas.

His minimalistic approach was sufficiently intriguing for Martin to be selected to exhibit in the survey show of British painting 'From Here' (1995) at both Karsten Schubert and Waddington Galleries. Later that year Martin was among a more focused selection of British painters who exhibited in 'Real Art' at Southampton City Art Gallery, a show which placed him alongside the other artists of his generation who now lead a new movement in reflexive painting. Also in 1995, Martin won the Sohen Ryu Tea Ceremony Foundation scholarship in Kamakura, Japan, and again exhibited in the Lisson Gallery's summer survey show, 'Postscript'. The following year saw another British painting show, 'About Vision', this time at the Museum of

Modern Art, Oxford, where Martin's two paintings, *Geronimo* and *Shaman* – each large-scale, singe-stroke works – stood out through their simplicity and sheer physicality.

Barrett

LONDON 1995. *From Here*, exhibition catalogue by Andrew Wilson, Waddington and Karsten Schubert galleries, London, 1995.
SOUTHAMPTON 1995. *Real Art. A New Modernism. British Reflexive Painters in the 1990s*, exhibition catalogue by Brian Muller, Southampton City Art Gallery, 1995.
Andrew Wilson, 'The Vision Thing', *Art Monthly*, January 1997.

Alain Miller | Born London, 1963

In 1996 Alain Miller produced a series of smiley-face paintings. However, on Miller's canvases the two dots that make the eyes and the slash that signifies the smile were replaced by water droplets painted on grey backgrounds. The face no longer smiled: tears replaced its eyes and a sagging, melancholic droop replaced its smile. Miller's smiley faces were paradoxically sad, their features rendered in arrested liquid drops.

Miller also makes spare paintings of human-like skeleton-figures with an assortment of non-human parts. Heads are made from wasps' nests, apes, or are even doubled as both male and female. Limbs are twigs and plant stems, while hands and feet may be clothes pegs or bananas. In true 'Arcimboldesque' fashion, Miller puts a surreal spin on social Darwinism.

Eye Love Eye (1997, p. 125) was shown at the 'Dissolution' show at Laurent Delaye, London, in 1997. It is a disquieting picture of a human heart with gazing human eyes on each ventricle; its aortic arch and arteries suggest facial contours and hair. Similar in scope to the skeleton series, *Eye Love Eye* collapses physiognomy with physiology to create an uncanny (self-) portrait of an organ-faced man.

Alain Miller graduated from the Chelsea School of Art, as well as Goldsmiths College. In 1996 he had a one-person exhibition at Anthony Reynolds Gallery, London, and also participated in the 'Absolute Vision' show at the Museum of Modern Art, Oxford.

Bussel

Sarah Kent, 'Dissolution', *Time Out*, 12–19 March, 1997, p. 52.
Waldemar Januszczak, 'Something To Smile About', *The Sunday Times*, 7 April 1996.
Andrew Wilson, 'The Vision Thing', *Art Monthly*, 202, December/January 1996-7, pp. 7–9.

Ron Mueck | Born Melbourne, Australia, 1958

Ron Mueck started his professional career as a puppet-maker and puppeteer for Australian television. In the mid-1980s he began working for Jim Henson on *Sesame Street* and films such as *Labyrinth*. He then worked for himself, fabricating models for television and print advertising. His Rabelaisian figures were used in campaigns for air freshener, toilet paper, spirits and peanut butter. He has since given up the puppets and other commercial work to pursue sculpture.

In 1995 Mueck made a life-size, hyper-realistic sculpture of a young boy in Y-fronts for painter Paula Rego. The work, entitled *Little Boy/Pinocchio*, was used by Rego for a series of Disney-inspired painting that were exhibited at the Hayward Gallery, London. Since then, Mueck has made three *Big Baby* (1996–7) sculptures – two-foot high, fastidiously detailed infants that crawl or crouch down on the floor. With their fleshy, over-sized, porcelain-white bodies and large gazing eyes, they are at once calming and sinister.

All of Mueck's work is made from clay models that are then cast in fibreglass or silicone and resin. One of his most striking works to date is a three-foot long sculpture of his deceased father – *Dead Dad* (1996, p. 127). To commemorate his father's death, an event which he did not witness, Mueck created an exact replica of his father's naked corpse. This inescapably eerie sculpture shows every wrinkle and hair in full detail. But its most disconcerting element is its child-like size.

With unfailingly strict attention to detail, perspective and scale, Mueck continues to make his uncanny portraits. Recently he has created a rabid mongrel, a male angel and a self-portrait mask, and has plans to construct a 50-foot sculpture of his mother.
Bussel

Louise Bishop, 'Model Family', *Creative Review*, April 1997, pp. 36–8.
Shaun Phillips, 'Big Ron, Little Ron', *The Face*, June 1997, pp. 106–12.

Chris Ofili | Born Manchester, 1968

On completing his BA at Chelsea School of Art, London, in 1991, Chris Ofili went straight on to the MA course at the Royal College of Art. By the time that he was awarded his MA in 1993, Ofili had already been included in the 'Whitworth Young Contemporaries' shows of 1989, 1990 and 1991 (being a prizewinner in 1989), the 'BP Portrait Award' in 1990 and 1991 at the National Portrait Gallery, and had won a British Council Travel Scholarship to Zimbabwe, where he also exhibited.

It was in Zimbabwe that Ofili experienced what some might call 'a moment of clarity' – struck by the limits of his paintings, and in an effort to ground them physically in a cultural as well as natural landscape, he hit upon the idea of sticking elephant shit on to them. Soon after, in 1993, Ofili held two *Shit Sales*, one in Berlin and the other in Brick Lane market, London, exhibiting several balls of elephant shit in the context of the market. He also employed his distinctive materials in an underground advertising campaign by placing stickers bearing the words 'elephant shit' on London street furniture. His newly elevated profile helped him into the exhibitions 'To Boldly Go' (1993) at Cubitt Street Gallery, and the 'BT New Contemporaries' (1993–4).

By 1995 Ofili was recognised as one of the leading painters of his generation. In that year he had a solo show at Gavin Brown's Enterprise, New York, and also participated in 'Brilliant! New Art From London' at the Walker Art Center, Minneapolis. In 1996 he showed in 'About Vision' at the Museum of Modern Art, Oxford, and the 'British Art Show 4', as well as winning a Wingate Young Artist Award and a commission from Absolut Vodka.
Barrett

Stuart Morgan, 'The Elephant Man', *Frieze*, 15, 1994.
LONDON 1996. *The British Art Show 4*, exhibition catalogue by Richard Cork, South Bank Centre, London, 1996.
Godfrey Worsdale, 'Chris Ofili', *Art Monthly*, July 1996.

Jonathan Parsons | Born Redhill, Surrey, 1970

Graduating from the BA course at Goldsmiths College in 1992, Jonathan Parsons went on to exhibit in 'The Coventry Open' at the Herbert Art Gallery, Coventry, in the same year. However, it was not until 1996 that he finally took part in his first London shows: 'Every Now and Then' at Richard Salmon, and 'The City of Dreadful Night' at Atlantis, both curated by the art organisation Rear Window. The first exhibition gave a showing to Parsons's flag pieces, while the latter event saw his work *Carcass* (1995, p. 135) – a road map of Britain delicately dissected with a scalpel to remove all but the roads. This latticework of highways hangs limply, like drawn veins.

Also in 1996, Parsons exhibited at the Heber-Percy Gallery, Leamington Spa, in his first solo show. His next solo show – his first in London – was at Richard Salmon in the same year. Here was seen his work *Mask*, in which a roadway cat's-eye has been coated in gold to mimic the funerary masks of the Egyptians. His work was also included that year in the group show 'Plastic' at the Arnolfini Gallery,

Bristol. In 1997 pieces of his were again shown at Richard Salmon in the group show 'Light', and at the Architectural Association's 'Building Site' exhibition.

Barrett

Mark Currah, 'Every Now and Then', *Frieze*, June 1994.

Rob Kesseler, 'City of Dreadful Night', *Untitled*, Spring 1995.

LONDON 1996. *Jonathan Parsons*, exhibition catalogue by Tom Shaw and Paul Heber-Percy, Richard Salmon Gallery, London 1996.

Richard Patterson | Born Leatherhead, Surrey, 1963

Richard Patterson makes large, anti-heroic, abstract paintings of minotaurs and motorcrossers that are less about their ostensible subject-matter than about painting itself. It is the paint rather than the image that establishes the works' register of metaphors – painterly strategies and the representation of paint and gesture are the focus of Patterson's art.

For both his motorcrosser and minotaur series, the artist used cheap plastic miniatures as models and then painted them to monumental scale on canvas. The works are at once painterly and photographic: there is little trace of brushstroke on their vividly colourful, almost airbrushed surfaces, yet at first glance they seem demonstratively gestural. Patterson's paintings are, in fact, visual tropes of the gestural.

Patterson has created paintings in which the figures are 'embellished' with bits of accidental paint from his studio. With great technical aplomb, Patterson paints the materiality of paint itself. Subject and representation endlessly mirror one another in works such as *Motorcrosser II* (1995, p. 140) or *Blue Minotaur* (1996, p. 137), which incorporate the very stuff of painting – the paint splatter on the miniatures – as their subject-matter.

Richard Patterson graduated from Goldsmiths College in 1986, and participated in Damien Hirst's 'Freeze' exhibition of 1988. In 1995, he had a one-person show in the Project Space at Anthony d'Offay Gallery, London. He has recently exhibited work at the British School at Rome, the Museum of Modern Art, Oxford, and the Hayward Gallery in London.

Bussel

Norbert Wilson, 'Open Plan', *The Royal Academy Magazine*, Autumn 1996, pp. 60–3.

Richard Shone, 'London and Edinburgh Contemporary Exhibitions', *Burlington Magazine*, August 1996.

Andrew Wilson, 'Gerhard Richter, Richard Patterson', *Art Monthly*, July 1995.

Simon Patterson | Born Leatherhead, Surrey, 1967

When he graduated from the BA course at Goldsmiths College in 1989, Simon Patterson had already participated in the now-legendary, Damien Hirst-curated exhibition 'Freeze' (1988). His distinctive working methods – taking an ordering system that exists within the world and applying it to another set of subjects – quickly became recognised as producing works that were theoretically compelling, at the same time as accessible and witty. Classic examples are his *Great Bear* (1992, p. 143), in which the London Underground map was remade with the names of famous people replacing those of the stations (on the Philosophers Line, the Footballers Line etc.), and the self-explanatory *Last Supper Arranged According to the ... Flat Back Four Formation (with Jesus Christ in Goal)*.

Patterson has gone on to exhibit in prestigious group shows such as 'Doubletake' (1992–3) and 'Material Culture' (1997) at the Hayward Gallery, as well as the Venice Biennale's 'Aperto' section (1993). Also in 1993, Patterson produced *Roadworks* as part of a public art project in Givors, France. For this he painted Formula 1 road markings onto the town's main thoroughfare: the starting grid was alongside the speed restriction signs at the entrance to the town; the finish was, of course, at the point where the speed restrictions ended.

Notable solo shows have included Patterson's 'General Assembly' (1994) at the Chisenhale Gallery, and 'Midway' (1995) at the Atrium Gallery, Fukuoka, Japan. In 1996 his solo show at the Lisson Gallery included *Untitled*, constructed from specially manufactured sail riggings. This piece was also exhibited later that year in the Tate Gallery when Patterson was shortlisted for the Turner Prize.

Barrett

Michael Archer, 'Jesus Christ in Goal', *Frieze*, 8, 1993.

LONDON 1994. *General Assembly*, exhibition catalogue by Patricia Bickers, Chisenhale Gallery, London, 1994.

Ian Hunt, 'Simon Patterson', *Art Monthly*, April 1996.

Hadrian Pigott | Born Aldershot, 1961

Ten years before finishing his studies at the Royal College of Art in 1993, Hadrian Pigott completed a degree in geology at Exeter University. This training instilled in him an interest in stratification and chemical processes, which in turn led him to begin producing ceramics. His eventual technical proficiency in this craft won him his place at the RCA, though he transferred to the sculpture department for his final year.

In 1993, Pigott was a prizewinner in the 'Whitworth Young Contemporaries' exhibition in Manchester. The following year saw him selected for the more prestigious 'BT New Contemporaries'. His work *Instrument of Hygiene (case 1)* (1994), first seen in Rear Window's 'Works Perfectly' exhibition, examines the collective psychology of society through the use of an everyday material: soap. Pigott is preoccupied by the paradox of the Western consumerist obsession with cleanliness, which yet leads to the increasing use of detergents that are far more toxic than bodily grime could ever be. His increasing fascination with soap led him to produce works that became ubiquitous in 1994 through his participation in such touring shows as Sarah Staton's 'Supastore Boutique' and the Arts Council's 'Art Unlimited: Multiples of the '60s & '90s'. That year also saw his first solo show, at Jibby Beane. Pigott went on to exhibit in other touring shows, including 'Fetishism: Visualising Power and Desire' (organised by the South Bank Centre) and 'Now Wash Your Hands' (both in 1995), and 'ACE!' (touring from 1996–7). Recently, Pigott has pursued the homely rituals of ablution deep into the terrain of sexual psychology and fetishism, as in his film *Dream*, in which a sink's overflow hole is soaped up and fondled past lather point.

Barrett

LONDON 1994. *Works Perfectly*, exhibition catalogue by Lynn MacRitchie, Rear Window, London, 1994.

David Barrett, 'Soap & Water: Profile on Hadrian Pigott', *Art Monthly*, February 1995.

LONDON 1995. *Fetishism: Visualising Power and Desire*, exhibition catalogue by Roger Malbert, South Bank Centre, London, 1995.

Marc Quinn | Born London, 1964

Marc Quinn graduated from Cambridge University in 1985. His work concerns the body in transformational, and at times conflicted states. Prior to the early 1990s Quinn made a series of busts out of bread dough that he baked and then cast in bronze, exploiting the unpredictability of his raw material to create contorted portraits of historical figures such as Marie Antoinette.

In 1991, Quinn exhibited *Self* (p. 147) at Jay Jopling/Grob Gallery, London, a work which brought him widespread recognition. Over a five-month period Quinn had eight pints of blood extracted from his body (the average amount in the human body), which he then poured into a cast of his head, froze and placed in a perspex cube attached to a refrigeration unit. Inspired by a cast of William Blake's face, *Self* is a meditation on mortality, tenuously held in frozen animation.

Emotional Detox: The Seven Deadly Sins (1995) was exhibited at the Tate Gallery, London. Consisting of a group of seven fragmented torsos cast in lead from Quinn's own body, this work is an exploration of the split between mind and body, between emotional and physical pain. In the same year Quinn produced *The Blind Leading the Blind*, a cast lead sculpture of the artist's body, cut off at the knees, head thrown back in elation, with the chest cavity exposing the sculpture's armature: a self-portrait of spiritual and physical ecstasy.

Quinn has shown widely in Britain, Europe and the United States. He was selected for the Sidney Bienniale in 1992, and participated in the 'Thinking Print' show at the Museum of Modern Art, New York, in 1996. In 1997 he is exhibiting at South London Gallery and at the Kunstverein in Hannover, Germany.

Bussel

Sarah Kent, *Shark Infested Waters: The Saatchi Collection of British Art in the 90s*, London, 1994.

Jane Rankin-Reed, 'Bad Blood', *Art + Text*, January 1993, pp. 26–8.

Marc Sanders, 'Invasion of the Body Sculptures', *Dazed and Confused*, 13, 1995, pp. 42–5.

Fiona Rae | Born Hong Kong, 1963

Fiona Rae graduated from Goldsmiths College in 1987. She participated in Damien Hirst's 'Freeze' exhibition the following year, was then picked up by London's prestigious Waddington's Gallery, and has since become one of the most successful artists of her generation.

Rae's large, vividly coloured abstract paintings question their own existence. They are frenzied amalgams of painterly gestures and styles quoted from the history of modern art and pop culture – from Picasso to Mickey Mouse. The paintings seek to resolve the conflict between pure abstraction and figurative representation in the age of postmodern appropriation. However, Rae's work does not so much discredit the Modernist myth of originality as provide a forum for a new voice: her own invented, hybrid language on the canvas.

As such, the paintings are playfully exuberant 'landscapes' rather than solemn art-historical conceits, a postmodern comedy of errors in drips, blobs, tangles and waves that is more *Hellzapoppin* than *Pulp Fiction*. Over the past few years, Rae's canvases have grown less discordant as her figures and forms have become more integrated and unidentifiable. In *Untitled (Parliament)* (1996), a black and white ground resembling formica provides a tenuous substratum for floating and disappearing discs painted in muted purples, yellows and greens. Smeared black and white bars penetrate in between, continuously disrupting all visual moorings.

Rae was shortlisted for the Turner Prize in 1991. In 1997 she had an exhibition at the Saatchi Gallery, London, and has recently had one-person shows at Contemporary Fine Arts, Berlin, and the British School in Rome.

Bussel

James Hall, 'Fiona Rae', *Artforum*, February 1996, p. 94.

LONDON 1997, *Fiona Rae and Gary Hume*, exhibition catalogue by Sarah Kent, Saatchi Gallery, London, 1997.

NEW YORK 1994. *Fiona Rae*, exhibition catalogue with essay by Emma Dexter, John Good Gallery, New York, 1994.

James Rielly | Born Wrexham, Wales, 1956

James Rielly paints intimate portraits of unknown people, people without names or histories. In the early 1990s he made paintings by manipulating found images from medical books, newspapers and magazines. Using pigment mixed with graphite, these canvases have a pale, ephemeral quality. This was mirrored by Rielly's subjects – missing or unidentified persons, ciphers for absence and alienation. The canvas became a memorial of sorts, the paintings evoking partial memories of misplaced narratives.

By 1995 a shift was discernible in Rielly's work. People now appeared as disfigured mutants: grainy pastel-coloured two-headed girls with men's faces, a fat boy with two sets of arms, or twin boys with four eyes each. Painted in a *faux-naïf* style under a pearlised veneer, the work is playfully sinister, suggesting the family portrait gone awry. For Rielly, it is in childhood that gender and society meet, and where abnormality becomes the norm.

Random Acts of Kindness (1996, p. 157) is a salon-style grouping of 40 small canvases. We see close-ups of a man's almost-severed head, a hand holding out a cocktail of pills, a family portrait with children exposing their knickers, an exhibitionist in the park. Painted in benign pinks, blues and yellows, Rielly's hilariously grotesque side-show of freaks is not a critique of society's victims but a compassionate plea on their behalf.

James Rielly received his MA degree from Belfast College of Art in 1981. In 1995 he was MOMART Fellow at the Tate Gallery, Liverpool. He has recently had one-person shows at the Musée des Beaux-Arts de Nantes and at Laurent Delaye, London.

Bussel

Charles Hall, 'James Rielly', *Untitled: A Review of Contemporary Art*, 6, 1994.

Sarah Kent, 'James Rielly', *Time Out*, 3–10 July 1996.

LIVERPOOL 1995. *Making It: Process and Participation*, exhibition catalogue, Tate Gallery, Liverpool, 1995.

Jenny Saville | Born Cambridge, 1970

In 1990, midway through her BA course at the Glasgow School of Art, Jenny Saville exhibited in 'Contemporary '90' at the Royal College of Art. In 1992 she completed her degree as well as showing in Edinburgh and in 'Critics Choice' at the Cooling Gallery, London. Following the success of her show at the Saatchi Gallery in 1994, which generated a great deal of publicity for her work (the images were ubiquitous that year), Saville went on to take part in the exhibition 'American Passion', which toured from the McLellan Gallery, Glasgow, to the Royal College of Art and the Yale Center for British Art in New Haven, Connecticut.

By 1994 many people were familiar with Saville's massive paintings, such as *Plan*, in which a naked woman is seen from below, her body filling the canvas through a combination of physical bulk and extreme foreshortening. Contour lines, as would demarcate the changes in altitude of land masses on a map, are drawn across the surface of the woman's skin. Saville's increasingly high profile enabled her to exhibit in several shows during 1996: 'Art On' in Halmstadt, Sweden; 'SAD' at Gasworks, London; 'Closed Contact: A Collaboration' at the Pace McGill Gallery, New York; 'Bad Blood' at the Glasgow Print Studio; and 'Contemporary British Art' at 'Art 96' in Stockholm. In 1997 Saville's work will appear in 'From the Interior' at Kingston University.

Barrett

Marsha Meskimmon, 'Women's Self-Portraiture, Exploration of Body', in *The Art of Reflection*, London 1996

Sarah Kent, *Shark Infested Waters: The Saatchi Collection of British Art in the 90s*, London, 1994

Alison Rowley, 'Generations and Geographies: Critical Theories' in *Critical Practices on Feminism and the Visual Arts*, edited by Griselda Pollock, London 1997

Yinka Shonibare | Born London, 1962

Yinka Shonibare completed his MA at Goldsmiths College in 1991, following three years at the Byam Shaw School of Art. He contributed work to the 'Interrogating Identity' exhibition that toured the USA in 1991 and in the following year was selected for the high-profile 'Barclays Young Artist Award', exhibited at the Serpentine Gallery, London. In 1994 he showed at the Bluecoat Gallery, Liverpool, in 'Seen/Unseen', as well as in 'TENQ' in Senegal, West Africa. By then his particular style – painting onto highly patterned African fabrics instead of primed canvas – had become well known, so much so that in the following year he was included in 'The Art of African Textiles' at the Barbican Centre, London.

Shonibare has continued to exhibit as much abroad as in the UK, in 1996 taking part in 'Inclusion : Exclusion' at Steirischer Herbst in Austria, the 'Tenth Biennale of Sydney' in Australia, as well as 'Out of Order', which showed at both the IAS, London, and the Cornerhouse, Manchester. 'Imagined Communities', organised by the Hayward Gallery as a National Touring Exhibition, brought his work to a wide audience across Britain, while 1997 has seen him selected for both the 'Johannesburg Biennale' in South Africa, and the large, as yet untitled survey show of British art that is to happen at the Museum of Contemporary Art in Sydney, Australia. He also had his first solo show in London in 1997, at the Stephen Friedman Gallery.

Barrett

LONDON 1996. *Out of Order*, exhibition catalogue by Stuart Morgan, IAS, London, 1996.
Kobena Mercer, 'Art That is Ethnic in Inverted Commas', *Frieze*, November 1995.
David Burrows, 'Pledge Alliegiance to a Flag?', *Art Monthly*, February 1997.

Jane Simpson | Born London, 1965

Jane Simpson recasts common domestic objects into uncommon forms: shelves, tables, chairs, ice-cream cones and kitchen utensils are her models. The resultant sculptures take on a new objecthood and, in the process, new meanings.

Simpson reproduces items of furniture and kitchenware in rubber that is then physically manipulated, made out-of-proportion, coloured or subjected to extremes of heat and ice. Her sculptures are rendered physically unstable through freezing and/or warming produced by hidden refrigeration units and light bulbs that control and preserve the work.

In Between (1993), a tongue-like shelf made of butter and brass, is at once frozen and melted by refrigeration and the heat from a light bulb; always in a state of flux, its colouration changes every day when the piece is turned on. *Table* (1996) is a rectangular dining-table bearing dishes, cups, utensils, a wine glass and a Chinese take-away box cast in aluminium. A white tablecloth hides a refrigeration unit that produces a thin skin of ice over all the objects and tabletop, transforming a domestic tableau into an uncanny frozen still-life.

In addition to the refrigeration sculptures, Simpson uses rubber to fabricate objects such as bar stools, stacked side tables and ice-cream cones that are contorted – almost 'melted' – abject likenesses of their former selves.

Jane Simpson graduated from the Chelsea School of Art, London, in 1988, and then attended the Royal Academy Schools. She participated in the exhibition 'Some Went Mad, Some Ran Away', curated by Damien Hirst at the Serpentine Gallery, London, in 1994, and recently had a solo show at Laurent Delaye Gallery, London.

Bussel

James Hall, 'Jane Simpson', *Artforum*, February 1997.
Marc Jancou, 'Lydia Dona and Jane Simpson', *Time Out*, 18–23 November, 1994.
Sarah Kent, *Shark Infested Waters: The Saatchi Collection of British Art in the 90s*, London, 1994.

Sam Taylor-Wood | Born London, 1967

Sam Taylor-Wood received her BA from Goldsmiths College in 1990. Her work incorporates aspects of photography, film, video installation and sound, in what has been described as an 'art-film hybrid'. In the early 1990s, Taylor-Wood produced a series of photographs using herself as a model. These were edgy provocations that questioned the limits of representation and artistic practice. *Gestures Towards Action Painting* (1992) is a parody of Hans Namuth's photographs of Jackson Pollock at work in his studio. This time the canvas is camouflage and the blurred figure is Taylor-Wood. In works such as *Slut* (1993) and *Fuck Suck Spank Wank* (1993) we see the artist 'revealed', exposed by an unknown narrative.

With *16mm* (1993) Taylor-Wood made a shift in medium to film installation. This work depicts a young woman in camouflage trousers and a white shirt dancing, or perhaps being made to dance, to the sound of invisible machine-gun fire. This piece was followed by *Killing Time* (1994), exhibited at The Showroom, London, in which isolated characters in a four-screen video projection face the camera and mime the lyrics to an opera soundtrack, trapped in their own narcissistic boredom. Since 1995 Taylor-Wood has produced a series of 'audio-photographs' entitled *Five Revolutionary Seconds* (pp. 170–1), recently shown at La Fundacio 'la Caixa' in Barcelona. Shot with a camera that makes a single image through a 360° turn, these elongated photographs, like a giant frieze, are populated by characters in a film-like scenario about which we know little. The only clues are the 'soundtrack' of overheard voices, the actors' poses, and the interior spaces they inhabit.

In 1996 Taylor-Wood premiered her six-screen synchronised panoramic video projection at Chisenhale Gallery, London. She has shown at White Cube, London, participated in the 'Life/Live' show at the Musée d'Art Moderne in Paris, and recently won an award for the most promising young artist in the 'Future, Present, Past' exhibition at the Venice Biennale, 1997.

Bussel

Daniel Birnbaum, 'Sam Taylor-Wood', *Artforum*, November 1996, pp. 88–9.
Gregor Muir, 'Sam Taylor-Wood', *Frieze*, 27, April 1996, pp. 79–80.
LONDON 1996. Sam Taylor-Wood, *Pent-Up*, exhibition catalogue, Chisenhale Gallery, London and Sunderland City Art Gallery, 1996.

Gavin Turk | Born Guildford, 1967

Gavin Turk was denied an MA certificate by the Royal College of Art in 1991. For his degree show he hung a fake English Heritage blue plaque on the wall that read: 'Borough of Kensington Gavin Turk Sculptor Worked Here 1989–1991', while his studio space remained conspicuously empty. By beginning his career with its metaphoric completion – in effect memorialising it – Turk announced his artistic programme: a critique of authorship and the myth of 'the artist' within the history of the European avant-garde.

In the early 1990s Turk made paintings based on his own signature: self-reflexive comments on the value of an artist's name, as well as the authority of his own. With *Piero Manzoni* (1992), Turk plagiarised the Italian artist's signature and then signed his own name to authenticate the work. *Stain* (1992), a work consisting of Turk's signature on a strategically stained piece of paper, is a wry commentary on Giacometti's habit of signing the used tablecloth in lieu of payment for a restaurant meal. Here again Turk questions the signature as a mark of worth and authenticity.

In 1993 Turk exhibited his sculpture *Pop* (p. 175) at a hired space in London through dealer Jay Jopling for a show entitled 'Collected Works 1989–1993'. The piece is a life-size waxwork portrait in a vitrine of Gavin Turk as Sex Pistol Sid Vicious appropriating the posture of Warhol's painting of Elvis as an armed cowboy. As a

continuation of Turk's self-memorialising plaque, *Pop* announces the metaphoric death of the artist and, by extension, of the avant-garde through its parody of 'the artist' as an embalmed pop icon.

In 1995 Turk participated in 'Young British Artists III' at the Saatchi Gallery, London. He recently showed a customised black-glossed skip entitled *Pimp* in the 1997 'Material Culture' exhibition at the Hayward Gallery, London.

Bussel

James Roberts, 'Last of England', *Frieze*, 13, November/December 1996, pp. 28–31.
LONDON 1993. *Gavin Turk, Collected Works 1989–1993*, exhibition catalogue, Jay Jopling, London, 1993.
Andrew Wilson, 'London Summer Round-Up', *Art Monthly*, 159, September 1992, pp. 18–19.

Mark Wallinger | Born Chigwell, 1959

Mark Wallinger was selected to show at the ICA as part of the 'New Contemporaries' exhibition in 1981, the year he graduated from the Chelsea School of Art. Two years later he presented his first solo show at The Minories, Colchester, and joined the MA course at Goldsmiths College. On finishing this course in 1985, Wallinger participated in the group shows 'Prelude' at Kettle's Yard, Cambridge, and 'New Art 2' at Anthony Reynolds Gallery, where he presented a solo show, 'Hearts of Oak', the following year. Further group shows followed at the Serpentine Gallery, London, and in the USA (the touring 'New British Painting' exhibition). 'Capital', his 1991 show, was seen at the Grey Art Gallery in New York as well as at the ICA and Manchester City Art Gallery.

Wallinger's 'Fountain' (1992) and 'The Full English' (1994) shows were both presented at Anthony Reynolds Gallery, before his large-scale solo show was seen at the high-profile Ikon, Birmingham, and Serpentine Galleries. Solo shows in 1997 have included 'Animal' at the CCA Glasgow, and 'God' at Anthony Reynolds Gallery, as well as the Deweer Art Gallery in Otogem, Belgium, and the Jiri Svetzka Gallery in Prague.

Group shows that Wallinger has contributed to in Britain over the last few years include 'Every Now and Then', 'Here and Now', 'The Art Casino', 'The British Art Show 4', and 'Offside! Contemporary Art and Football'. In 1995 he was nominated for the Turner Prize, the year after he had presented his racehorse, *A Real Work of Art*, as a real work of art.

Barrett

Adrian Searle, 'Fools and Horses', *Frieze*, January 1993.

Paul Bonaventura, 'Turf Accounting: Profile on Mark Wallinger', *Art Monthly*, April 1994.

Jon Thompson, *Mark Wallinger*, exhibition catalogue, Ikon Gallery, Birmingham, Serpentine Gallery, London, 1995.

Gillian Wearing | Born Birmingham, 1963

Gillian Wearing is interested in the fears, fantasies and secrets of ordinary people, and in how we, as spectators of her work, identify with them. Her work seeks to unveil the psychical register of identity through the lens of subjective realities by creating a context for people to speak, to be seen and to act out. Wearing uses photography and video in her collaborative projects to ascertain how through self-expression (or confession) individuals inscribe themselves into a common social fabric.

In 1992 Wearing embarked on a project entitled *Signs that say what you want them to say and not signs that say what someone else wants you to say.* She asked anonymous people on the street to write whatever was on their mind, using identical paper signs and markers. The photographs show people with signs that read: 'I'm desperate', 'Will England get through the recession', or 'Come back Mary, I love you'. Since then, Wearing has made video works of people singing along to their favourite songs on a Walkman; men and women acting out their cowboy fantasies in costume, shown at the Hayward Gallery; and people in disguise relating their innermost secrets.

Wearing has also used herself in her work, as in the photo series *Take Your Top Off* (1993), in which she posed naked in bed with naked transsexuals, or *Dancing in Peckham*, for which she danced in the middle of a shopping mall without any music as confused passers-by looked on.

10 - 16 (1997, p. 181) is a video installation of seven films in which adult actors lip-synch the voices of children interviewed by Wearing. The characters reveal thoughts that range from unselfconscious innocence to unmediated evil.

Gillian Wearing graduated from Goldsmiths College in 1990. In 1997 she had solo shows in London at Chisenhale Gallery and Interim Art, at the Kunsthaus, Zurich, and Emi Fontana, Milan.

Bussel

Gregor Muir, 'Sign Language', *Dazed and Confused*, 25, December 1996, pp. 52–5.

Adrian Searle, 'Gillian Wearing', *Frieze*, 18, September/October 1994, pp. 61–2.

Gilda Williams, 'Wearing Well', *Art Monthly*, 184, March 1995, pp. 24–6.

Rachel Whiteread | Born London, 1963

Rachel Whiteread makes sculptures of the negative spaces of common domestic objects. Her work literally solidifies the absence of the object – whether it be a room, a house, a chair, a bathtub or a hot-water bottle – making it into a tangible, material thing. With the opacity or luminescence of plaster, rubber or resin, the sculptures create an iconography of memory and loss. They are the negative imprint, both relic and residue, of something that once was, their surfaces still showing legible traces of the object from which they were cast. Twice removed from their origin, they are both ghostly fossils and physical embodiments of ossified, negative space.

In 1990 Whiteread made *Ghost* (pp. 184–5), a mausoleum-like cube cast from a Victorian room, which evoked collective memories of a childhood past. Three years later she gained international fame with *House*, a plaster cast of the outside of an East London council house. Resembling an abstract Modernist sculpture, *House* sought to memorialise the ideals of government housing and was a monument to the failed project of post-war social architecture.

In tandem with her large-scale pieces, Whiteread has also cast familiar domestic objects such as sinks, tables and book shelves. *Untitled (100 Spaces)* (1995, pp. 188–9) is an installation of 100 green, amber or yellow translucent resin sculptures of the spaces beneath chairs and stools. A common bathtub, *Untitled (Orange Bath)* (1996, p. 187), is simultaneously transformed into a coffin and a vibrant life-retaining receptacle.

Rachel Whiteread graduated from the Slade School of Fine Art in 1987, and has since become one of the most successful artists of her generation. In 1993 she was awarded the prestigious Turner Prize. In 1997 she became the first woman to exhibit on her own as the British representative at the Venice Biennale. She won a competition for the Judenplatz Holocaust Memorial in Vienna, but recently withdrew following controversy and hostile publicity. Whiteread has also had solo shows at the Tate Gallery, Liverpool, and at the Reina Sofia, Madrid.

Bussel

Mark Cousins, 'Inside outcast', *Tate*, 10, Winter 1996, pp. 36–41.

Sarah Kent, *Shark Infested Waters: The Saatchi Collection of British Art in the 90s*, London, 1994.

LIVERPOOL 1997. *Rachel Whiteread: Shedding Life*, exhibition catalogue with essays by Rosalind Krauss, Bartomeu Mari, Stuart Morgan, Michael Tarantino, Tate Gallery, Liverpool, 1997.

Cerith Wyn Evans | Born Llanelli, Wales, 1958

Cerith Wyn Evans graduated from the Royal College of Art in 1984. He began his career as a video- and film-maker and worked as an assistant to Derek Jarman. During the 1980s Wyn Evans made short experimental films that have been screened in Britain and abroad. He has also collaborated with choreographer Michael Clark, and was a Tutor at the Architectural Association in London for six years.

In the early 1990s Wyn Evans gave up film-making for sculpture and installation. His work deals with the phenomenology of time, language and perception. In 1996 he created an installation at White Cube, London, entitled *Inverse, Reverse, Perverse* (p. 191). This consisted of a large concave mirror hung on the gallery wall that inverted and radically distorted the viewer's reflection, producing a disturbing self-portrait. He also placed over the door of the exhibition space a back-to-front green neon exit sign, *TIX3* (1994), that when reflected in the mirror further displaced the viewer's sense of perceptual limits.

For the 'Life/Live' show at the Musée d'Art Moderne, Paris, Wyn Evans created a site-specific, 40-metre-long wall-text in fireworks. Its title, *In Girum Imus Nocte Et Consumimur Igni* (1996), is a Latin palindrome that refers to a film by the French Situationist Guy Debord. The text itself is by Karl Marx and reads: 'Better that the whole world be destroyed and perish utterly than that a free man should refrain from one act to which his nature moves him'. Here, the cultural devaluation of revolutionary discourse was contrasted with the fireworks' suspended potential to explode.

In 1995 Wyn Evans participated in the 'General Release' show at the Venice Biennale. In 1997 he exhibited at the Hayward Gallery in London, the British School in Rome, and had a one-person show at Deitch Projects in New York.

Bussel

LONDON 1997. *Material Culture: The Object in British Art of the 1980s and '90s*, exhibition catalogue, Hayward Gallery, London, 1997.

Jerry Saltz, 'Cerith Wyn Evans', *Time Out New York*, 80, 3–10 April 1997, p. 40.

Mark Sladen, 'Cerith Wyn Evans', *Frieze*, 30, September/October 1996, p. 75.

Contemporary British Art

Matthew Collings, *Blimey! From Bohemia to Britpop: The London Artworld from Francis Bacon to Damien Hirst*, London 1997

Sarah Kent, *Shark Infested Waters: The Saatchi Collection of British Art in the 90s*, London 1994

J. Lingwood (ed.), *House*, London 1995

LONDON 1988. *Freeze*, exhibition catalogue by Damien Hirst, Surrey Docks, London 1988

LONDON 1990. *Modern Medicine*, exhibition catalogue by Billee Sellman, Carl Freedman and Damien Hirst, Building 1, Drummond Road, London SE16, London 1990

LONDON 1990. *Gambler*, exhibition catalogue by Billee Sellman and Carl Freedman, Building 1, Drummond Road, London SE16, London 1990

LONDON 1991. *Broken English*, exhibition catalogue by Andrew Graham-Dixon, Serpentine Gallery, London 1991

LONDON ET AL. 1994–5. *Some Went Mad, Some Ran Away...*, exhibition catalogue by Richard Shone, Serpentine Gallery, London 1994; Nordic Arts Centre, Helsinki, 1994; Kunstverein, Hannover 1994; Museum of Contemporary Art, Chicago 1995

LONDON 1996. *Chapmanworld*, exhibition catalogue with essays by David Falconer, Douglas Fogle and Nick Land, ICA, London 1996

LONDON 1997. *Fiona Rae and Gary Hume*, exhibition catalogue by Sarah Kent, Saatchi Gallery, London 1997

LONDON 1997. *Material Culture: The Object in British Art of the 1980s and '90s*, exhibition catalogue by Michael Archer and Greg Hilty, Hayward Gallery, London 1997

MINNEAPOLIS AND HOUSTON 1995–6. *Brilliant! New Art from London*, exhibition catalogue by Douglas Fogle, Walker Art Center, Minneapolis 1995–6; Contemporary Art Museum, Houston 1996

Andrew Renton (ed.), *Technique Anglaise: Current Trends in British Art*, with Liam Gillick and Damien Hirst, London and New York 1991

The Broader Picture

Michael Archer, *Art Since 1960*, London 1997

Arthur C. Danto, *After the End of Art: Contemporary Art and the Pale of History*, Princeton University Press, Princeton 1997

Hal Foster, *The Return of the Real: The Avant-Garde at the End of the Century*, Cambridge, Massachusetts 1996

LONDON 1987. *New York Art Now*, exhibition catalogue by Dan Cameron, Saatchi Gallery, London 1987

Nicolas de Oliveira, Nicola Oxley and Michael Petry, *Installation Art*, with texts by Michael Archer, London 1996

Irving Sandler, *Art of the Postmodern Era: From the Late '60s to the early '90s*, New York 1996

Donald Kuspit, *Signs of Psyche in Modern and Postmodern Art*, New York 1996

List of Works

Darren Almond

1. **A Bigger Clock** | 1997
steel, perspex, aluminium, paint, motor
154 x 206 x 98 cm 60.5 x 81 x 38.5 in
(p. 51)

2. **Fan** | 1997
wood, plastic, micro-processors, paint, motors
diameter 450 cm 177 in

Richard Billingham

3. **Untitled** | 1993
colour photograph on aluminium
105 x 158 cm 41.3 x 62.2 in
(p. 53)

4. **Untitled** | 1995
colour photograph on aluminium
105 x 158 cm 41.3 x 62.2 in
(p. 54, above)

5. **Untitled** | 1995
colour photograph on aluminium
105 x 158 cm 41.3 x 62.2 in
(p. 54, below)

6. **Untitled** | 1993
colour photograph on aluminium
120 x 80 cm 47.2 x 31.5 in
(p. 55, above)

7. **Untitled** | 1994
colour photograph on aluminium
80 x 120 cm 31.5 x 47.2 in
(p. 55, below)

8. **Untitled** | 1995
colour photograph on aluminium
105 x 158 cm 41.3 x 62.2 in
(p. 56, above)

9. **Untitled** | 1995
colour photograph on aluminium
80 x 120 cm 31.5 x 47.2 in
(p. 56, below)

10. **Untitled** | 1995
colour photograph on aluminium
158 x 105 cm 62.2 x 41.3 in
(p. 57)

Glenn Brown

11. **The Day the World Turned Auerbach** | 1992
oil on canvas
56 x 50.5 cm 22 x 19.9 in
(p. 59)

12. **Dali-Christ** | 1992
oil on canvas
274 x 183 cm 107.9 x 72 in
(p. 60)
'Dali-Christ' 1992 after 'Soft Construction with Boiled Beans' 1936 by Salvador Dali. By kind permission of DEMART PRO ARTE BV for this.
© Glenn Brown 1992

13. **Ornamental Despair (Painting for Ian Curtis) After Chris Foss** | 1994
oil on canvas
201 x 300 cm 79 x 118 in
(p. 61)

Simon Callery

14. **Newton's Note** | 1996
oil on canvas
255 x 320 cm 100.4 x 126 in
(p. 63)

Jake & Dinos Chapman

15. **Great Deeds Against the Dead** | 1994
mixed media with plinth
total: 277 x 244 x 152 cm 109 x 96 x 59.8 in
(p. 65)

16. **Ubermensch** | 1995
fibreglass, resin, paint
366 x 183 x 183 cm 144 x 72 x 72 in
(p. 66)

17. **Zygotic acceleration, biogenetic, de-sublimated libidinal model (enlarged x 1000)** | 1995
fibreglass
150 x 180 x 140 cm 59 x 70.9 x 55.1 in
plinth: 180 x 20 x 150 cm 70.9 x 7.9 x 59 in
(p. 67)

18. **Tragic Anatomies** | 1996
fibreglass, resin, paint, smoke devices
varied measurements
(pp. 68–9)

Adam Chodzko

19. **The God Look-Alike Contest** | 1992–3
(Last Judgement Version)
mixed media
57 x 44.5 x 2.5 cm each 22.4 x 17.5 x 1 in
(p. 71)

Mat Collishaw

20. **Bullet Hole** | 1988–93
cibachrome mounted on 15 light boxes
229 x 310 cm 90 x 122 in
(p. 73)

Keith Coventry

21. **White Abstract (Sir Norman Reid Explaining Modern Art to the Queen)** | 1994
oil on canvas, wood, gesso, glass
66 x 105 x 7.2 cm 27.5 x 43.75 x 3 in
(p. 75)

Peter Davies

22. **Text Painting** | 1996
acrylic on canvas
203 x 254 cm 79.9 x 100 in
(p. 77)

23. **Small Squares Painting** | 1996
acrylic on canvas
365.8 x 238.8 cm 144 x 94 in

Tracey Emin

24. **Everyone I Have Ever Slept With 1963–1995** 1995
appliquéd tent, mattress, light
122 x 245 x 214 cm 48 x 96.5 x 84.3 in
(p. 79)

Paul Finnegan

25. **Untitled** | 1995
mixed media, shoes
185 x 140 x 90 cm 72.8 x 55.1 x 35.4 in
(p. 81)

Mark Francis

26. **Negative** | 1995
oil on canvas
244 x 214 cm 96 x 84.3 in
(p. 83)

27. **Elements** | 1996
oil on canvas
213.4 x 183 cm 84 x 72 in

Alex Hartley

28. **Untitled (Ronan Point)** | 1995
black-and-white photograph, MDF, steel
200 x 90 x 35 cm 78.7 x 35.4 x 13.8 in
(p. 85)

29. **Untitled** | 1995
plinth, acrylic, photograph
60 x 30 x 27 cm 23.6 x 11.8 x 10.6 in;
plinth: 85 x 120 x 85 cm 33.5 x 47.2 x 33.5 in

Marcus Harvey

30. **Proud of His Wife** | 1994
oil and acrylic on canvas
198 x 198 cm 78 x 78 in
(p. 88)

31. **Myra** | 1995
acrylic on canvas
396 x 320 cm 156 x 126 in
(p. 87)

32. **Dudley, Like What You See? Then Call Me**
1996
acrylic on canvas
198 x 198 cm 78 x 78 in
(p. 89)

Mona Hatoum

33. **Deep Throat** | 1996
table, chair, television set, glass plate, fork,
knife, water glass, laser disc, laser disc player
74.5 x 85 x 85 cm 29.3 x 33.5 x 33.5 in
(p. 91)

Damien Hirst

34. **A Thousand Years** | 1990
steel, glass, flies, maggots, MDF, insect-o-cutor,
cow's head, sugar, water
213 x 427 x 213 cm 84 x 168 x 84 in
(p. 94)

35. **The Physical Impossibility of Death in the Mind of Someone Living** | 1991
tiger shark, glass, steel, 5% formaldehyde
solution
213 x 518 x 213 cm 84 x 204 x 84 in
(p. 93)

36. **Isolated Elements Swimming in the Same Direction for the Purpose of Understanding**
1991
MDF, melamine, wood, steel, glass, perspex cases, fish, 5% formaldehyde solution
183 x 274 x 30.5 cm   72 x 108 x 12 in
(p. 94)

37. **Away from the Flock** | 1994
steel, glass, lamb, formaldehyde solution
96 x 149 x 51 cm   38 x 59 x 20 in
(p. 98)

38. **Argininosuccinic Acid** | 1995
gloss household paint on canvas
335 x 457.2 cm   132 x 180 in
(p. 95)

39. **Some Comfort Gained from the Acceptance of the Inherent Lies in Everything** | 1996
steel, glass, cows, formaldehyde solution
12 tanks: each 200 x 90 x 30 cm
78.7 x 35.4 x 11.8 in
(pp. 96–7)

40. **This little piggy went to market, this little piggy stayed at home** | 1996
steel, GRP composites, glass, pig, formaldehyde solution, electric motor
2 tanks: each 120 x 210 x 60 cm
47.2 x 82.7 x 23.6 in
(p. 98)

41. **beautiful, kiss my fucking ass painting**
1996
gloss household paint on canvas
diameter 213.4 cm   84 in
(p. 99)

Gary Hume

42. **Dolphin Painting No IV** | 1991
gloss paint on MDF board
4 panels, total: 222 x 643 cm 87.4 x 253.1 in
(pp. 102–3)

43. **Begging For It** | 1994
gloss paint on panel
200 x 150 cm 78.7 x 59 in
(p. 101)

44. **Tony Blackburn** | 1994
gloss paint on panel
194 x 137 cm 76 x 54 in
(p. 104)

45. **Vicious** | 1994
gloss paint on panel
218 x 181 cm 86 x 71 in
(p. 105)

46. **My Aunt and I Agree** | 1995
gloss paint on aluminium panel
200 x 1100 cm 79 x 433 in
(pp. 106–7)

Michael Landy

47. **Costermonger's Stall** | 1992–7
wood, gloss paint, tarpaulin, plastic buckets, electric lights, flowers
182.8 x 213.3 x 213.3 cm 71.9 x 83.9 x 83.9 in
(p. 109)

Abigail Lane

48. **Blue Print** | 1992
chair with felt ink pad seat, blue ink, framed print
122 x 46 x 91 cm 48 x 18 x 36 in

49. **Misfit** | 1994
wax, plaster, oil paint, human hair, clothing, glass eyes
60 x 85 x 192 cm 23.5 x 33.5 x 75.5 in
(p. 111)

Langlands & Bell

50. **Ivrea** | 1991
hardwood, wood products, glass, cellulose lacquer
total: 160 x 500 x 18 cm 63 x 196.9 x 7.1 in
(p. 113)

51. **The House of Arabs** | 1990
MDF, beech, wood products, glass, lacquer
total: 180 x 220 x 15 cm 71 x 87 x 6 in

Sarah Lucas

52. **Sod You Gits** | 1990
photocopy on paper
216 x 315 cm 85 x 124 in
(p. 118)

53. **1 – 123 – 123 – 12 – 12** | 1991
size seven boots with razor blades
(p. 117)

54. Figleaf in the Ointment | 1991
plaster, hair
lifesize
(p. 117)

55. Receptacle of Lurid Things | 1991
wax
lifesize
(p. 117)

56. Two Fried Eggs and a Kebab | 1992
photograph, fried eggs, kebab, table
76.2 x 152.4 x 89 cm   30 x 60 x 35 in
(p. 116)

57. Au Naturel | 1994
mattress, water bucket, melons, oranges,
cucumber
83.8 x 167.6 x 144.8 cm   33 x 66 x 57 in
(p. 115)

58. Where Does It All End? | 1994–5
wax and cigarette butt
6.4 x 9.5 x 6.4 cm   2.5 x 3.75 x 2.5 in
(p. 117)

59. Bunny | 1997
tights, plywood chair, clamp, kapok stuffing
with wire
101.5 x 90 x 63.5 cm   40 x 35.5 x 25 in
(p. 119)

Martin Maloney

60. Sony Levi | 1997
oil on canvas
173.5 x 298 cm   68.3 x 117.3 in
(p. 121)

61. Sleeping Arrangements | 1997
oil on canvas
167.5 x 297 cm   65.9 x 116.9 in

Jason Martin

62. Geronimo | 1996
oil on canvas
274.5 x 274.5 cm   108 x 108 in

63. Merlin | 1996
oil on aluminium
244 x 244 cm   96 x 96 in
(p. 123)

Alain Miller

64. Eye Love Eye | 1997
oil on canvas
235 x 195 cm   92.5 x 76.75 in
(p. 125)

Ron Mueck

65. Dead Dad | 1996–7
silicone and acrylic
20 x 102 x 38 cm   7.75 x 40 x 15 in
(p. 127)

66. Pinocchio | 1996
polyester resin, fibreglass and human hair
84 x 20 x 18 cm   33 x 8 x 7 in

Chris Ofili

67. Spaceshit | 1995
oil paint, polyester resin, map pins, elephant
dung on linen
183 x 122 cm   72 x 48 in
(p.129)

68. Afrobluff | 1996
acrylic paint, oil paint, paper collage, polyester
resin, map pins, elephant dung on linen
243.8 x 182.9 cm   96 x 72 in
(p. 132)

69. Afrodizzia | 1996
paper collage, oil paint, glitter, polyester resin,
map pins, elephant dung on linen
243.8 x 182.9 cm   96 x 72 in
(p. 130)

70. Popcorn Tits | 1996
oil paint, paper collage, glitter, polyester resin,
map pins, elephant dung on linen
183 x 122 cm   72 x 48 in
(p. 131)

71. The Holy Virgin Mary | 1996
paper collage, oil paint, glitter, polyester resin,
map pins, elephant dung on linen
243.8 x 182.9 cm   96 x 72 in
(p. 133)

Jonathan Parsons

72. Achrome | 1994
sewn polyester flag with rope and toggle
457 x 228.5 cm   179.9 x 90 in

73. **Carcass** | 1995
dissected map in acrylic case
200 x 110 x 40 cm 78.7 x 43.3 x 15.7 in
(p. 135)

Richard Patterson

74. **Motorcrosser II** | 1995
oil and acrylic on canvas
208 x 315 cm 82 x 124 in
(p. 140)

75. **Blue Minotaur** | 1996
oil on canvas
208 x 312.4 cm 82 x 123 in
(p. 137)

76. **Culture Station #2 – Dirty Picture** | 1996
oil on canvas
213.3 x 427.7 cm 84 x 168.3 in
(pp. 138–9)

77. **Culture Station #3 – With Fur Hat** | 1997
oil on canvas
213.3 x 427.7 cm 84 x 168.4 in
(p. 141)

Simon Patterson

78. **The Great Bear** | 1992
four-colour lithographic print in anodised
aluminium frame
109 x 134.8 x 5 cm 42.9 x 53 x 2 in
(p. 143)

Hadrian Pigott

79. **Instrument of Hygiene (case 1)** | 1994
fibreglass, leatheret covering, velvet lining,
with wash basin and fittings
90 x 50 x 43 cm 35.4 x 19.6 x 16.9 in
(p. 145)

Marc Quinn

80. **Self** | 1991
blood, stainless steel, perspex, refrigeration
equipment
208 x 63 x 63 cm 82 x 25 x 25 in
(p. 147)

81. **The Morphology of Specifics** | 1996
glass and silver
dimensions variable
(p. 148)

82. **No Visible Means of Escape** | 1996
RTV 74-30, rope
180.3 x 59.7 x 30.5 cm 71 x 23.5 x 12 in
(p. 149)

Fiona Rae

83. **Untitled (one on brown)** | 1989
oil on canvas
213.4 x 198 cm 84 x 78 in
(p. 155)

84. **Untitled (purple and brown)** | 1991
oil and charcoal on canvas
198 x 213.4 cm 78 x 84 in
(p. 154)

85. **Untitled (blue and purple triptych)** | 1994
oil on canvas
183 x 502.9 cm 72 x 198 in
(pp. 152–3)

86. **Untitled (Sky Shout)** | 1997
oil and acrylic on canvas
274.3 x 243.8 cm 108 x 96 in
(p. 151)

James Rielly

87. **Random Acts of Kindness** | 1996
oil on canvas
overall size 410 x 290 cm 161.4 x 114.1 in
(p. 157)

Jenny Saville

88. **Propped** | 1992
oil on canvas
213.5 x 183 cm 84 x 72 in
(p. 159)

89. **Plan** | 1993
oil on canvas
274 x 213.5 cm 108 x 84 in
(p. 161)

90. **Trace** | 1993–4
oil on canvas
213.5 x 182.8 cm 84 x 72 in
(p. 160)

91. **Shift** | 1996–7
oil on canvas
330 x 330 cm 130 x 130 in
(p. 163)

92. **Hybrid** | 1997
oil on canvas
274.3 x 213.4 cm 107.9 x 84 in
(p. 162)

Yinka Shonibare

93. **How Does a Girl Like You, Get to Be a Girl Like You?** | 1995
wax print cotton textiles
168 x 40 cm approx 66 x 15.8 in
(p. 165)

Jane Simpson

94. **Sacred** | 1993
MDF, gesso, watercolour, tinplate, refrigeration unit
112.5 x 127.5 x 55 cm 48 x 50 x 22 in
(p. 167)

Sam Taylor-Wood

95. **Killing Time** | 1994
video projection and sound (60 minutes)
dimensions variable
(p. 169)

96. **Five Revolutionary Seconds I** | 1995
colour photograph
21 x 200 cm 8.3 x 78.7 in
(pp. 170–1)

97. **Wrecked** | 1996
C-type colour print
152.4 x 396.2 cm 60 x 156 in
(pp. 172–3)

98. **Five Revolutionary Seconds III** | 1996
colour photograph
20.5 x 200 cm 8 x 78.7 in
(pp. 170–1)

99. **Five Revolutionary Seconds VII** | 1997
colour photograph
29.5 x 200 cm 11.6 x 78.7 in
(pp. 170–1)

Gavin Turk

100. **Pop** | 1993
glass, brass, MDF, fibreglass, wax, clothing, gun
279 x 115 x 115 cm 110 x 45 x 45 in
(p. 175)

101. **Cave** | 1991–5
ceramic plaque
diameter: 49 cm 19.2 in

Mark Wallinger

102. **Race Class Sex** | 1992
oil on canvas
each: 230 x 300 cm each: 90.5 x 118 in
(pp. 178–9)

103. **Angel** | 1997
video/laserdisc
duration: 7 minutes 30 seconds
(p. 177)

Gillian Wearing

104. **10 - 16** | 1997
video projection
duration: 15 minutes, dimensions variable
(p. 181)

Rachel Whiteread

105. **Ghost** | 1990
plaster on steel frame
269 x 355.5 x 317.5 cm 106 x 140 x 125 in
(pp. 184–5)

106. **Untitled (Square Sink)** | 1990
plaster
107 x 101 x 86.5 cm 42 x 40 x 34 in
(p. 186)

107. **Untitled (Bath)** | 1990
plaster, glass
103 x 105.5 x 209.5 cm 40.5 x 41.5 x 82.5 in
(p. 183)

108. **Untitled (One-Hundred Spaces)** | 1995
resin
100 units, dimensions variable
(pp. 188–9)

109. **Untitled (Orange Bath)** | 1996
rubber, polystyrene
80 x 207 x 110 cm 31.5 x 81.5 x 43.3 in
(p. 187)

Cerith Wyn Evans

110. **Inverse Reverse Perverse** | 1996
surface mirrored acrylic
diameter: 73 cm 28.7 in
(p. 191)

Brooks Adams is a Contributing Editor of *Art in America* and the author of many reviews, articles and essays on modern and contemporary art, including 'Notes on Camelot: The 1960s', for the Royal Academy's 1993 exhibition 'American Art of the Twentieth Century'; and 'Like Smoke: A Duchampian Legacy' for 'The Age of Modernism: Art in the 20th Century', a 1997 exhibition at the Martin-Gropius-Bau in Berlin. He lives in New York and is married to the writer and critic Lisa Liebmann.

David Bussel is a writer and art critic based in New York and London. He received an MA in Comparative Literature from the City University of New York in 1996, and has written for *Frieze*, *Flash Art* and *Interview* magazines.

David Barrett is an artist and writer based in London. He completed three years of study at the Byam Shaw School of Art in 1994, and contributes regularly to *Frieze* and *Art Monthly* magazines. In 1995 Barrett began a two-year MA course at the Slade School of Fine Art, during which time he contributed essays for various exhibition catalogues, including the forthcoming publication *Space Explorations*.

Lisa Jardine is Professor of Renaissance Studies at Queen Mary and Westfield College, University of London, and an Honorary Fellow of King's College, Cambridge.

Martin Maloney is an artist, critic and curator. He writes regularly for *Art Forum* and *Flash Art* magazines and lectures in fine art at Goldsmiths College, London.

Norman Rosenthal has been Exhibitions Secretary of the Royal Academy of Arts, London, for the past twenty years. Since 1974 he has organised a number of survey exhibitions on the art of the 20th century in co-operation with Christos M. Joachimides, including 'Art into Society – Society into Art' (London, 1974), 'A New Spirit in Painting' (London, 1981), 'Zeitgeist' (Berlin, 1982), 'German Art in the 20th Century' (London and Stuttgart, 1985–6), 'Metropolis' (Berlin, 1991), 'American Art in the 20th Century' (Berlin and London, 1993), and 'The Age of Modernism. Art in the 20th Century' (Berlin, 1997).

Richard Shone, an associate editor of *The Burlington Magazine* since 1979, is the author of several books, including *Bloomsbury Portraits* (1976), *Century of Change: British Painting since 1900* (1977), *Walter Sickert* (1988) and *Sisley* (1992). In 1992 he was co-selector of 'Sickert' at the Royal Academy of Arts, London. He has written catalogue essays for exhibitions by, among others, Ian Davenport, Abigail Lane, Damien Hirst, Rachel Whiteread and Fiona Rae, and wrote the essays for *Some Went Mad, Some Ran Away* (1994) and *Made in London* (1996). He was on the jury for the 1987 Turner Prize and the purchasing committee of the Arts Council Collection between 1994 and 1996, and was a selector for 'New Contemporaries' (1996).

Photographic Credits